PROMOTION AND TENURE

SUNY Series
FRONTIERS IN EDUCATION
Philip G. Altbach, Editor

The Frontiers in Education Series draws upon a range of disciplines and approaches in the analysis of contemporary educational issues and concerns. Books in the series help to reinterpret established fields of scholarship in education by encouraging the latest synthesis and research. A special focus highlights educational policy issues from a multidisciplinary perspective. The series is published in cooperation with the School of Education, Boston College. A complete listing of books in this series can be found at the end of this volume.

PROMOTION AND TENURE

Community and Socialization in Academe

William G. Tierney

and

Estela Mara Bensimon

STATE UNIVERSITY OF NEW YORK PRESS

Published by
State University of New York Press

For information, address the State University of New York Press,
State University Plaza, Albany, NY 12246

Production by Bernadine Dawes • Marketing by Dana Yanulavich

Library of Congress Cataloging-in-Publication Data

Tierney, William G.
    Promotion and tenure : community and socialization in academe /
William G. Tierney and Estela Mara Bensimon.
        p.   cm. — (SUNY series, frontiers in education)
    Includes bibliographical references and index.
        ISBN 0-7914-2977-6 (hc : alk. paper). — ISBN 0-7914-2978-4 (pbk. : alk. paper)
        1. College teachers—Tenure—United States.   2. College teachers—Promotions—
United States.   3. Professional socialization—United college teachers—United States.
4. Minority college teachers—United States.   5. Women college teachers—United
States.   I. Bensimon, Estela Mara.   II. Title.   III. Series.
LB2335.7.T54   1996
378.1'22—dc20   96-10349
                                                                                              CIP

1   2   3   4   5   6   7   8   9   10

For Elinor Richardson

Contents

Acknowledgments

We are deeply indebted to the professors, department chairs, and academic leaders who participated in the study. Without their cooperation and their willingness to be open about what often proved to be sensitive topics of conversations, this project would not have been possible. We are also grateful to our campus liaisons for their assistance in scheduling our interviews and providing us with institutional materials. Because we promised participants anonymity we cannot recognize them by name here, nor can we name the institutions that welcomed us. Even so, we wish to express our gratitude for their participation.

We are particularly indebted to professors Beverly Guy-Sheftall, Spelman College, and Anne Austin, Michigan State University, for their willingness to read the manuscript and provide us with many suggestions for improvement. We are also grateful to other colleagues who at various stages of the project provided us with advice and shared with us their work and ideas, among them professors Deborah Atwater, Penn State University, Robert Boice, SUNY at Stoney Brook, and Esther Rothblum, University of Vermont.

We owe special thanks to several colleagues and graduate students who consistently offered us outstanding research support. Rebecca Kline conducted interviews at one of the institutions in our sample; both Joanne Gainen and Rebecca Kline assisted us in developing materials for a Junior Faculty Institute held at the 1994 annual meeting of the American Educational Research Association; Andres Bolanos served as graduate assistant during the life of the project and managed the editorial process. We also thank Kent Keith. Don Braswell, as always, provided superb editorial assistance. We also wish to acknowledge the involvement of Sheila Petrosky, staff assistant at the Center for the Study of Higher Education, who managed the administrative aspects of the project as well as the final preparation of the manuscript.

Over the years Peggy Heim, formerly a program officer with TIAA-CREF, has been extremely supportive of our work. We are grateful to her and TIAA-CREF for providing us with assistance for the project's dissemination activities.

Lastly we wish to express our thanks to the Lilly Endowment for its generous support of this study and to Ralph Lundgren, who served as program officer for this project.

PROMOTION AND TENURE

CHAPTER 1

Community and Culture in Academe

Bad News

On a humid summer evening, about twenty individuals have assembled at Tony's home for a party. "I feel as if I'm going to a wake, not a party," murmurs Jane Riegal as she enters the house and makes her way to the back yard. The guest of honor, Fred, sits at the picnic table and appears to be engrossed in earnest conversation with one of his departmental colleagues. At no point during the evening does the party ever move above whispered dialogues. Finally, toward 10:00 P.M., Tony clears his throat and says, "I'd like to propose a toast." Everyone clusters around Fred, but most stare at the ground. "We wish Fred all the best in his new job and will miss him here for his wit and dedication to his students." Tony reaches for a laugh by saying, "I will also miss someone I could always beat on the squash court," but no one smiles. Fred nods a thank-you, and the crowd begins to break up and head home.

Everyone has gone now except Fred and Tony. Tony walks in and out of the house, peripatetically rearranging lawn chairs and tables as Fred stands awkwardly in the living room staring off into space. Finally he moves toward the door and says, "I had better be going, too." Tony stops picking up the discarded styrofoam cups and plates, but he cannot think what to say. Fred starts to sob, and Tony embraces him. "C'mon now. I'm sure it'll be okay. Forget this place." Fred weeps silently for a moment longer, then quietly says, "Thanks for the party. It was good to be able to say goodbye to everyone at once." After a pause, he continues:

> I feel like such a failure. I spent six years working my ass off and I never really thought they'd deny me tenure. I've been over this so many times it's ridiculous. My teaching was good. My service was good. Research was okay. Who do I blame? No one ever—EVER—said anything but good things to me. I get fucked over, and I just . . . I don't know. It just doesn't seem worth it. Getting that letter from the dean, everybody averting their eyes from me like I had a disease. I will never forget it. Never.

1

Fred's colleague, Jane Riegal, drives home from the party with her husband. Unlike Fred, Jane has been successful. After six difficult years, the university readily promoted her to associate professor this past spring. "Fred was treated unfairly," Jane explains to her husband, Johnny, "but he also never read the signals. He spent too much time worrying about students, and they gave him dopey committees to serve on. Bad move. And he has a way of saying things that set you on edge. You have to be political, and he's not." She shrugs her shoulders and settles into her seat, beginning to plan the vacation that she and Johnny will take next week.

This is the first summer since graduate school that Jane feels she has been able to breathe freely. She and Johnny will even take a two-week vacation. She has told more than one friend, "All I'm going to do is read trashy novels. I can't wait!" She has also mentioned to her best friend that she and Johnny are going to try to have a baby. They have wanted a child ever since graduate school, but the time has never been right. Jane was too busy for motherhood, and the department would have interpreted her pregnancy as a sign that she was not serious about her career. So she waited, and the two weeks on Fire Island seem an odd luxury. She reads her "trashy novels," and Johnny and she spend long afternoons in bed.

Jane also finds herself getting up an hour or two before Johnny and reading some articles for an NSF proposal she wants to write. At night, after Johnny falls asleep, she wonders about her life and its odd twists and turns. She's mastered the system and is proud of herself for having done so, but at times she also feels that something is missing. Her father was a professor, but her career is far different from what she remembers of his. The romance of being a professor, the excitement of engaging in ideas and the challenge of working with stimulating colleagues seems absent. She works in a hollow community, and even while she was telephoning friends and family about the good news of her tenure, she secretly felt that somehow she hadn't measured up to her ideal. Her ideas weren't good enough, perhaps; she wasn't adept at collegiality; maybe that was why she always felt lonely. That would account for the letdown feeling rather than elation when she received the tenure letter. She does not share her misgivings with anyone, not even Johnny. Eventually she drifts off to sleep and awakens to begin work on her proposal before the sun comes up.

Certainly no one other than Jane senses her discomfort in the department. Relationships are generally cordial and always restrained. The department chair says, "How terrific!" when she tells him she's pregnant. In the next breath he tells her, "The provost has asked me to suggest members for a Promotion and Tenure Review Committee. I gave him your name. You may get a call." A few days later, the provost's secretary calls to inform Jane that she has been appointed secretary of the committee. The provost comes to the first meeting in September and tells the group that he wants a study of how to improve promotion and tenure. "I really want to know what it's like in the trenches. What are the problems? What should we be doing? Pay particular attention to our minorities. Women, too. We need to do a good job, a better job, and I'm relying on this group for information."

The committee meetings take more time than Jane had anticipated, but she also enjoys the work. It is a university-wide group, and some senior faculty are involved. For the first time at the university, she feels as if colleagues are actually listening to what she has to say. The committee members have set various tasks for themselves, and because Jane has the most experience in survey research, she chairs the sub-committee that develops the questionnaire for all junior faculty. Others interview faculty members and departmental chairs. Throughout the year, she hears a great deal of gallows humor. "You won't believe this," says a friend who has been conducting interviews, and proceeds to tell another horror story from an untenured professor's point of view. The individuals in the group also feel that they have made progress, and as their April deadline approaches, they reach consensus about the kind of problems that exist and the recommendations that they will make to the provost.

Jane almost skips the May meeting with the provost because the baby is due in two weeks. However, she has heard so many snide comments during the year from colleagues hoping she could "keep up" that she overcompensates. By actual count Jane realizes that she had attended more committee meetings than Professor Allen, the endowed chair in chemistry, but no one has remarked on his absences. She arrives at the provost's office and settles into a chair at the oblong table.

When the provost enters, he is stone-faced and avoids eye contact:

> First, I need to thank you for this report. It clearly shows work. Hard work. I don't think we'll be able to use it, however, and I want to tell you why. I've found the method questionable, and I think if we gave it broad publicity, it would cause harm. The interviews strike me as impressionistic. They have an ax to grind. And the survey is too simplistic.
>
> It also contains too much bad news. The president hates whining, and this report is like that. Faculty feel overworked. Women feel excluded. Minorities serve on too many committees. This is a can of worms that we can't deal with at this time. But I'm sure we will. Eventually. But not now. I want to let you in on a secret. We're going to launch a capital campaign this summer

and we wouldn't want to start off with bad news, would we? We need good news. Like Professor Riegal's NSF grant. Congratulations!

Viewing Academe

If the research for this book is representative of what takes place on college campuses throughout the United States, then the above scenario is emblematic of commonplace occurrences in the late twentieth century. Some faculty feel isolated, and others never "learn the rules of the game." Administrators often want to hide "bad news," and others do not want to believe stories about life "in the trenches" that document overwork and stress for women and faculty of color. During a twenty-four month period that began in the fall of 1992, we conducted more than 300 interviews with faculty at twelve colleges and universities. Private and public institutions, research universities, liberal arts colleges, small, medium, and large institutions were included in the sample. The framework for promotion and tenure varies by institutional type, but we shall suggest in chapter 2 that the experiences, frustrations, and challenges of faculty members are often remarkably similar, yet paradoxically, an individual's or group's experiences are also unique.

Chapter 3 delineates the struggles that junior faculty face, and chapters four and five relate specific experiences of women and faculty of color. To be sure, an assistant professor at a small, private liberal arts college will teach more classes than his counterpart at a large, public research university. Similarly, a science professor will be more dependent on funds to equip and maintain a laboratory than her peers in the liberal arts and humanities. The argument we shall develop here, however, is that although the institutional and departmental contexts of one's work may vary, the cultural framework in which it is defined and performed is often quite similar across campuses and disciplines. The feeling of not fitting in experienced by a female professor, the volume of committee work assigned to an African-American assistant professor, or the pressure exerted on a new faculty member to publish are more than individual examples of what someone has encountered on the road to promotion and tenure at his or her own institution.

Common negative experiences are indications that the system is in need of change. Accordingly, in the final chapter we relate the data presented in the text to a theoretical framework we have developed in order to offer suggestions for reform. In this chapter we also offer very specific recommendations on how institutional leaders can improve the probationary period for tenure-track faculty.

Throughout this work, we portray the professional life of primarily one group of participants—junior faculty—in order to expose a system gone awry. By contrasting the comments of junior faculty with those of their senior colleagues, we reveal the competing definitions of reality held by different groups. We did not begin this study with the assumption that promotion and tenure should be abolished, nor will we conclude with such a recommendation. However, academe is in need of dramatic restructuring, and the data in this text are offered as evidence of why we call for change.

In what follows, we outline three interpretations of the present state of the academy and give particular attention to their ramifications for promotion and tenure. Our point here is that the beliefs one holds about the academy inevitably frame how one acts in a postsecondary institution. Far too often, the actors in an institution believe that there is only one possible interpretation of the organization. Consequently, decisions are made in an instrumental fashion with neither a vision of what could be nor an understanding of the cultural context in which the institution exists.

Postsecondary institutions most certainly exist in the real world and have real problems. Reduced revenues from the federal and state governments have played havoc with fiscal planning. Minority candidates for faculty positions are still relatively few in the number pool, especially in the sciences and engineering. On many campuses, the physical plant is in dire need of renovation simply to remain functional. Different constituencies—state legislators, businesses, parents, accrediting agencies—often have competing demands about what they want to see taking place on campus. The collegiality and social fabric that characterized colleges and universities have been torn asunder by daily acts of divisiveness and rancor by virtually every constituency on campus.

On one level, such statements are difficult to challenge. College financing is in dire straits, so consequently deferred maintenance is commonplace. Only four percent of U.S. doctorates were earned by African Americans in engineering in 1993 (National Research Council 1993). Although the style of college protests may differ from that of the Vietnam era, no one argues that faculty, students and administrators have less regard for one another. However, as we explain below, a cultural view of the world takes such facts as statements that demand interpretation.

Upon receiving the report about promotion and tenure, the provost in the initial scenario regarded it strictly as bad news. Bad news of this kind had to be suppressed, for it presented the institution in a negative light.

Another possibility might have been to use the document as a point of departure for rethinking the promotion and tenure process. Still another option might be to consider whether the current faculty workload is actually the best use of faculty time.

Ultimately, these issues are philosophical in nature: What should be the role of the faculty vis-à-vis society? How should academic freedom be defined? What roles do promotion and tenure play in protecting academic freedom? And yet, we seldom deal with such questions in a philosophical manner that might help to give meaning to our lives; rather, such questions are seen as instrumental and political topics. Faculty need more mentoring, the thinking goes, so develop a mentoring system. If the state legislature finds out that we are not hiring a sufficient number of minority faculty members, goes another line of thought, it might reduce appropriations even further. We had better bury the offending document.

Regrettably, this line of reasoning appears to make sense on one level. State legislatures do often meddle in the internal affairs of institutions. The rush of daily events often forces administrators to make spur-of-the-moment decisions rather than long-range ones, so a stopgap program for mentoring is quickly put in place without reconsidering how junior and senior faculty might work together most effectively. Although we understand why the participants in an institution might (or might not) adopt particular policies, we are concerned that academe is not confronting these issues forthrightly with creative and far-reaching analyses.

In what follows, we offer three competing views of the world—conservative, liberal humanist, and critical postmodernist—to illustrate different approaches to academe's ills. We are particularly concerned with delineating the ramifications of each view for the promotion and tenure system. Variations of the first two approaches are the most common ways that organizations function. We first sketch these world views and then critique them. Then we develop the approach to be used throughout the remainder of the text—critical postmodernism.

A Conservative View of the Academy

Beginning in the 1980s and continuing to the present, there has been a succession of well-publicized critiques of academic life by individuals who consider themselves conservatives. Ronald Reagan's Secretary of Education, William Bennett, for example, criticized higher education as being out of touch with the mainstream and having lost its sense of purpose, in large part, because too many faculty presented their "subjects in a tendentious, ideological manner" (1984, 16). The University of Chicago's Allan Bloom contended that in the 1960s faculty and administrators had let reason fall by the wayside as they abdicated their "higher vocation" and allowed "a highly ideologized student populace" to take over (1987, 313). The consequence of the infusion of ideology into the curriculum, argue the conservatives, is that institutions are no longer able to claim that they teach students about truth, freedom, and justice. In his analysis of Duke University, Dinesh D'Souza observed, "The real question is whether, as a liberal arts university, Duke will continue to uphold principles of justice and excellence, or whether those principles will be casually jettisoned for the unabashed pursuit of power and expediency" (1991, 193). The conservative perspective suggests that those who "jettison" such principles are primarily the faculty, with the willing compliance of administrators and the unwitting acceptance of the student body.

Roger Kimball's book *Tenured Radicals* also follows this line of thought, but from his perspective, the war has been waged and his side has lost. Writing of leftist faculty members who have taken over the university, he contends "their dreams of radical transformation have been realized" (1990, xiv). In essence, Bloom's "highly ideologized" student populace has been transformed. Writes Kimball:

> When the children of the sixties received their professorships and deanships they did not abandon the dream of radical cultural transformation; they set out to implement it. Now, instead of disrupting classes, they are teaching them; instead of attempting to destroy our educational institutions physically, they are subverting them from within. (1990, 167)

What are the implications for the curriculum if we adopt the conservative agenda? How might we assess student learning from this perspective? Should a tuition policy that enables many low income students to attend college be reconfigured if those students are not as well prepared as the traditional students and compel the institution to debase the curriculum? Although these are interesting subjects of debate, for the purposes of this text we focus on two other questions raised by the conservative critique: (a) what is the portrait of faculty that has been developed, and (b) what does such a description suggest about the promotion and tenure process? Not only are these questions germane to the topic of this book, but the conservatives would also argue that if we answer them, then solutions to other problems, such as student access or institutional accountability, can be found.

In general, the conservative critique of faculty is twofold. On one hand, professors are characterized as largely ideological and radical, and on the other, they are depicted as disengaged intellectuals who prefer to conduct esoteric research rather than teach undergraduate courses. At times these images converge and complement each other, and at other times they are described in isolation. They are never contradictory, however. Conservatives do not contend that all faculty members are radical, but nevertheless they are overly concerned with excellence in college teaching. Similarly, faculty are never described as conducting vital research, but they are invariably accused of not paying attention to teaching. In the conservative framework faculty are parodied as misanthropes who want to be left alone to develop obscure theories that are ideologically tainted (Sykes 1988).

While it would be an overstatement to imply that the conservative critique suggests that all faculty behave in this manner, it also would be incorrect to say that we have reduced the conservative portrait of the faculty to mere caricature. Bennett, Bloom, Kimball and others (Ravitch 1990, Sowell 1992, Sowell 1993) have portrayed the faculty—especially those in the humanities and social sciences—as deserving of societal disdain and disapproval. They have abnegated their responsibility as purveyors of Truth and Reason and, in doing so, now "express lack of interest, if not contempt, for the Western classics" (D'Souza 1991, 255). Similarly, faculty have driven up the cost of higher education by their selfish desire to conduct research. As Thomas Sowell trenchantly observes, all teaching is disdained by faculty—not just the Western classics—and the citizenry end up paying for "the many new boondoggles thought up by the faculty" (1992, 24) who neglected their primary purpose of educating the young.

The promotion and tenure system is criticized indirectly as being flawed. That is, conservatives in general do not call for restructuring the promotion and tenure process; rather, they view the process as having been corrupted by ideologues. Indeed, the title of Kimball's book, *Tenured Radicals*, proclaims the dangers of the promotion and tenure system. Presumably, if there were merely radicals in academe, they could be removed, but because they have tenure, they have been able to take over the academy. Of consequence, a professor is "blissfully unaware of how privileged and protected a position he and his colleagues occupy in society, thanks precisely to their being insulated" (1990, 184). Tenure allows isolation.

In a curious twist, the promotion and tenure system has also come to subvert what it was created to protect: academic freedom. If one of the reasons for the creation of tenure was to protect faculty so that they could engage in intellectual battle without fear of reprisal, then that purpose has been lost. The conservative argument is that the system has been taken over by leftists, and if a faculty member does not walk the ideological line, he or she will be at risk of not attaining promotion and tenure. The academy has become a McCarthyite nightmare where it is not unusual to inquire, "Are you now or have you ever been conservative" (Kimball 1990, 172). According to the conservative view, the problem is not only that ideologues have taken over a rational process that once protected academic freedom, but also that younger faculty members who must go through the process are socialized to think that this is the norm. As with today's students who are deprived of the knowledge that previous generations derived from reading the classics, today's junior faculty are also losers because they are no longer able to work in a system where the battle for Truth is of paramount importance.

One final observation about the conservative critique is that its proponents offer only the most general solutions to complex problems. In large part, the lack of clear-cut solutions is a result of the problem: the faculty. The promotion and tenure system itself is not so much at fault as are the individuals who control the process. Those who control the dialogue are responsible for the bastardization of the curriculum or the lack of standards in academe. Thus, implicitly, the conservative critique revolves around the ability to purge the universities of radical riff-raff. If the academy had better faculty members—as defined by the conservatives—then its current malaise could be overcome.

Part of the success of the conservative agenda has been the clarity and uniformity with which its proponents have promulgated their interpretation of academic life. While conservatives may disagree with one another on minor points, their similarities are greater than their differences. However, perhaps because of the stridency of their language and the lack of clear-cut solutions, the conservatives have garnered the most notoriety and least support. The "scorched-earth" rhetoric that the conservatives have employed often does not ring true for most academics, and their picture of the campus of the 1950s seems to be a romanticization of the past that can never be, and many believe should never be, recaptured. The colleges and universities of the twenty-first century will be technologically, socially, and culturally distinct from the academic institutions of yesteryear. The conservative yearning for college life as it was in the "good old days" is often based on a revisionist view of those times, and has little if anything to do with the educational needs of present and future generations.

A Liberal Humanist View of the Academy

In contrast to the conservative interpretation of the academic world, the liberal humanist view is less condemnatory of individuals and groups. It also relies less on analyses based on explicit political ideologies. We define this interpretation as "liberal humanist" because its proponents hold a traditional view of the academic world. Colleges and universities have long been, and still remain, devoted to the life of the mind. The triple functions of the university—research, teaching, and service—are still important. The relationship between society and the postsecondary institution has always been tenuous, and this will continue. Scholars need distance from the everyday world in order to deal with intellectual issues, yet it is their responsibility to provide creative ideas for dealing with social and environmental problems.

In contrast to the conservative's desire to preserve the academic community as a historical artifact, the liberal humanist hopes to maintain core values—academic freedom, for example—while adapting to meet the needs of society. Proponents of this latter view generally subscribe to the belief that cultural diversity is important and to be respected; even so, they bemoan the loss of community on college campuses. Although problems such as political correctness exist, the extent to which they have eroded academic life is seen as less devastating than the large scale cataclysm that the conservatives claim to be observing. In effect, liberal humanists admit that there are leftist ideologues in academe, but they see as much danger in crusades from the right as in indoctrination from the left.

If the problems that confront academe are not political in nature, then what are they? Academe has at least three interrelated problems pertaining to the scope of this text that must be resolved:

1. Undergraduate teaching is undervalued.
2. The social fabric of the academic community has been torn asunder.
3. Research is often irrelevant, and researchers are frequently disengaged from their own communities as well as from society at large.

In general, these problems are not viewed from the personal perspective favored by conservatives. Instead, rationales are offered about how we have arrived at a situation in which senior faculty may never teach a freshman seminar, or faculty of one department at a small liberal arts college may never get to know faculty of another department on the same campus.

Perhaps the chief proponent of the liberal humanist interpretation of academe is Ernest Boyer, president of the Carnegie Foundation. Drawing on the research of Eugene Rice, in *Scholarship Reconsidered*, Boyer does not place blame for the devaluation of undergraduate teaching, but instead he offers a historical analysis of how we have arrived at a system in which research is paramount in academe. He writes:

> Research *per se* was not the problem. The problem was that the research mission, which was appropriate for *some* institutions, created a shadow over the entire higher learning enterprise. . . . The emphasis on undergraduate education

. . . was being overshadowed by the European university tradition, with its emphasis on graduate education and research. . . . The focus had moved from the student to the professorate, from general to specialized education, and from loyalty to the campus to loyalty to the profession. (1990, 13)

Such a view largely coincides with analyses by other scholars such as Roger Geiger (1993) and Burton Clark. Clark writes, for example, that "the discipline rather than the institution tends to become the dominant force in the working lives of academics" (1983, 30). If this view is correct, then research—a disciplinary activity—takes precedence over the primarily institutional activities of teaching and service. In fact, research attained greater importance in the United States since the Second World War, and many believe that this has been at the expense of undergraduate teaching. James Fairweather (1993) has recently discussed the results of a national survey that pertains to the faculty reward structure. The results of the survey indicate that in every type of four-year institution, research is more highly rewarded—as defined by financial incentive—than any other activity. Thus, a professor in a public research university or a small private liberal arts college will derive greater rewards for conducting research than teaching undergraduates.

According to liberal humanists, the results are manifold. We have an undergraduate curriculum that is too often assigned to teaching assistants, and faculty devote much more of their time to research than to teaching. Many senior faculty no longer teach undergraduate seminars because they prefer to deal exclusively with graduate students. Moreover, large classes have become commonplace because the faculty would rather spend their time in front of their computers or in their labs than in the classroom.

Similarly, the campus has lost the flavor of being an academic community because the faculty find intellectual "homes" in their disciplines. Telecommunication has made conversation with one's disciplinary colleagues simple and straightforward, so faculty may now deal with their intellectual comrades rather than their institutional peers. The result is that conversations about the purpose of the institution, or dedication to the work and life of the campus has fallen into disfavor, if not disrepute.

Although one senses that liberal humanists are not unlike conservatives in their yearning for lost community, a key difference is that liberal humanists do not blame "the children of the sixties" for the present state of higher education. Instead, liberal humanists believe the reward structure has created the problem. The implications are clear. If the problem is with personnel, then the solution is to rid the academy of unsatisfactory faculty; if the problem is structural, then the structure itself must be reconfigured.

Boyer's book has been widely discussed in academic circles because he calls for academe to give higher priority to teaching, and to redefine research. "We believe the time has come," he states, "to move beyond the tired old 'teaching versus research' debate and give the familiar and honorable term 'scholarship' a broader, more capacious meaning" (1990, 16). He goes on to define scholarship as spheres of multidimensional excellence in which basic and applied research, integration and synthesis, and teaching are accorded equal importance. As opposed to the simplistic documentation of one's research efforts, Boyer calls for faculty portfolios that show how an individual is involved in each domain of scholarship. He also calls for greater differentiation across institutional types, so that the emphasis of a faculty portfolio in a research university will differ from that of one in a comprehensive institution.

Thus, liberal humanists differ in many ways from conservatives in their analyses and conclusion. All the ills of academe from the curriculum to access cannot be attributed to personnel problems. Indeed, liberal humanists vary in their interpretations of the problem, so that the clarity and simplicity of language that characterize the writings of conservatives is often absent from that of liberal humanists. For example, Boyer talks about the dilemma of teaching versus research, whereas Russell Jacoby emphasizes how academic intellectuals have privatized their language and excluded the public from discussion and debate (1987). Boyer's solution will not solve Jacoby's problem, and vice versa.

At the same time, liberal humanists see the world as defined by structural dilemmas that require creative solutions. Where the conservatives offer quasi-philosophical statements—"reading the classics is what ties civilization together"—liberal humanists offer quasi-practical solutions—"redefine the promotion and tenure system." While the conservatives have garnered most of the attention from the public at large, it is fair to say that the liberal humanists have received the most thoughtful consideration from within the academy.

A Critical Postmodern View of the Academy

In some respects, critical postmodernism is based on assumptions that are akin to the conservative and liberal humanist positions. Like the conservatives, critical postmodernists subscribe to an explicit political ideology, albeit a dramatically different one. Unlike the conservatives, they do not attribute the problem to individual actions and beliefs. Rather, like liberal humanists, critical postmodernists view the problems of academe as structural. They differ from their liberal humanist counterparts, however, by not interpreting structure simply as technical in nature, but as being rooted in ideology and culture. As critical postmodernism forms the scaffolding for our text, we take pains first to critique the other two approaches and then to delineate how one uses such a construct to analyze the problems and struggles faced by junior faculty.

The liberal humanist analysis of the rise of research and the devaluation of teaching is a point on which virtually all serious scholars of higher education concur. However, the liberal solution is technocratic in nature—change the structure of the way faculty work. From this perspective, organizations exist in ideological vacuums, and if one tinkers with the structure, then change will occur. Logically, approaches such as Total Quality Management (TQM) or a desire for better ways to assess and evaluate different activities have attained prominence.

The foregoing solution ignores the relationship between faculty work and knowledge production. The assumption is that the creation of knowledge is a neutral activity and that individuals discover knowledge in a systematic and objective way. Who discovers knowledge is irrelevant. That an individual is a man, an African American, or a lesbian should make no difference in terms of how one studies a particular area of knowledge. Individual difference is subjugated to communal norms, and common definitions of excellence, effectiveness, or even what qualifies as knowledge are accepted.

Colleges and universities, as institutions, are not placed within a cultural framework where symbols and ideology are in concert with structure. To their credit, liberal humanists have rejected the stark individualism that permeates the conservative critique, but in their search for technical solutions, they seem to have overlooked or ignored the deeper structure in which academe is situated. Instead, the participants in a postsecondary institution conform to specific norms that have accrued over time, and individuals who enter the organization simply must learn those norms. In effect, a standard is set, and successful socialization is defined by the ability of the individual to internalize, accept, and meet that standard.

Conservatives implicitly acknowledge the deeper structures to which we refer, but they do so in a manner that is hardly conducive to thoughtful dialogue. They argue that "leftist" ideas are ideological and therefore tainted, but firmly believe that their own ideas are neither ideological nor tainted. "Revolutionaries" have taken over the academy and replaced a value-neutral curriculum with a "politically correct" one. Where rational dialogue once reigned supreme, the thinking goes, only one line of thought is now allowed.

From a critical postmodern perspective, the problem with such an assertion is that knowledge is constructed. This being the case, it is inevitably related to larger ideological structures, whether on the left or the right. All

knowledge construction is political. All organizations exist in socially created spheres. In essence, liberal humanists avoid the discussion of ideology
entirely and assume that problems have technical solutions. Conservatives
bemoan the fact that ideology has entered the academy, and assume that if
we rid colleges and universities of those who brought it in, then institutions
of higher education will return to a level of excellence believed to have been
lost within living memory.

Curiously, both standpoints provide similar visions of the academic
community as it was in the past. It is remembered with nostalgia, and the
wish to return to it is often expressed. To be sure, liberal humanists would
like to reconstruct the academic community so that it is populated with a
more diverse group of individuals, but the desirability of the community
itself is unchallenged. In effect, they want different people brought into the
academy, but these individuals need to be assimilated. The academy should
serve as a melting pot par excellence, in that individuals will be judged by
their ideas and not who they are. As ideas, the rough and tumble of discrimination is avoided.

Both interpretations of academic community stem from the assumption
of unity. An academic community is formed around singular notions of what
constitutes knowledge, and its members interpret the world from a shared
conception of the purposes of higher education. From this perspective, the
breakdown of community may be decried or bemoaned, and academic poli-
cymakers must strive to regain what we once had. In this notion of the past,
students learned what was important, and faculty taught and conducted research on what was equally important.

Rejecting these assumptions, critical postmodernism posits a radically
different vision of academic community. For the purpose of this text, we
frame the interpretation of academic community from three perspectives:
intellectual, existential, and political-strategic. Why we define academic
community by way of intellectual, cultural and political perspectives will
become clear if we begin by outlining the background of critical theory and
postmodernism.

Briefly, we employ critical theory as an analytic tool in our effort to
understand the oppressive acts of society; the intent is to develop culturally-
based solutions to these problems. Culture neither equates with the technical
notion of structure of the liberal humanist, nor does it suggest that solutions
exist only through individual action. Instead, critical theorists seek to understand how ideology determines structure. *Ideology* is the set of doctrines
through which those in an organization make sense of their own experiences.
Culture is viewed as the manifold ways in which meaning is enacted; but it
is also the terrain on which meaning is defined. We seek to understand how

social groups make sense of their lives and circumstances. Culture is interpretive, the product of the social and ideological relations in which it is inscribed. Culture is neither passed down unproblematically from one generation to the next, nor is it static. Culture is changed as new individuals and groups enter into it, and it is transformed by present contexts and surrounding social life.

The culture of an organization is a contested area in which individuals and groups struggle over the definition of knowledge and what it means to be a knowledgeable individual. As opposed to a static concept that equates culture with the taxonomic parts of an institution, the idea advanced here is that culture is the product of the social relations of the participants within an organization. Ideologies of colleges and universities, then, both reflect and reform the beliefs of the society in which these institutions exist. Culture is a series of contested areas, discourses, and relations of power pertaining to the nature of reality.

From another angle, postmodernists challenge modernist notions of rationality, norms, and identity (Tierney, 1993a). They reject the notion that we can ever understand ultimate Truth through reason; instead, truth is considered ephemeral and subject to multiple, conflicting interpretations. Instead of having the critical theorists' goal of eliminating the oppressive acts of society, postmodernists seek to delineate the multivocal relations of power that exist in order to understand differences. As Henry Giroux notes, "By insisting on the multiplicity of social positions postmodernism has seriously challenged the political closure of modernism with its divisions between the center and the margins and in doing so has made room for those groups generally defined as excluded others" (1988, 166). Postmodernism is thus centrally concerned with decoding the multiple images that occur and brings into question previously unchallenged ideas about language and identity. Rather than assuming that community is good or bad, we investigate its meaning. Instead of operating with the idea that social identity exists as a unified entity, we search for the multiple constructions at work that contribute to the definition of self.

How might we use admittedly abstract theories to deal with life in academe? Luke and Gore answer this question with regard to feminist and critical theories:

> Classroom practice is ultimately linked to theories of the subject, the social, learning and teaching. . . . The differences between a [liberal humanist] and constructivist theory of gendered subjectivity has significant implications for the ways pedagogical relations can be conceptualized. In that regard, theoretical choice has important consequences for practice. And what some might call

the more esoteric concerns of poststructuralist feminisms form the very work which has opened up questions of representation, of voice, difference, power, and authorship-authority which are central to the politics of classroom practice. (1990, 193)

We agree; we also suggest that "theories of the subject" and the like have implications for multiple activities in academe and not only for "classroom practice." How critical postmodernists interpret the struggles that junior faculty face enables us to move beyond simple solutions that either blame individuals or seek to recreate idealized notions of lost communities. Taken together, critical theory and postmodernism imply that to understand the organization, we must come to terms with the multiple interpretations that exist about it. In particular, we need to come to terms with groups who differ from the norm—such as women and faculty of color. If reality is contested and interpreted, then we must understand how different groups define their multiple realities before we develop proposals for change or improvement.

Accordingly, we interviewed individuals in different institutions and from multiple standpoints, not to search for consensus, but rather to come to understand how they interpret their respective worlds. As we shall see, some individuals such as deans or provosts may dismiss such interpretations. "Junior faculty have it tough, and it's just something they have to get through," stated one academic administrator in an interview. "We all went through the initiation—you know how it is—and they just need to hold on, figure it out, and they'll see daylight." Such remarks reveal an assumption that we are all more or less alike. A conservative would want to know what the neophyte faculty are teaching or writing about to determine whether it is appropriate. A liberal humanist would seek to reorient the structure so that priorities might be reconfigured. Ultimately, however, neither approach encourages respect for differences of individuals and groups nor how differences are structured as negatives by taken-for-granted practices.

From the perspective advanced here, we seek to extend the idea of creating *communities of difference* in academe. In this light the central concept of critical postmodernism is a belief that difference is important, that organized change can occur, and that we must work toward the creation of a community that does not demand the suppression of one's identity in order to become socialized to abstract norms. We support the development of organizations in which interrelatedness and concern for others is central. A community of difference implies that the community is de-normed. In keeping with the ideas of critical theory, postmodernism, culture, and ideology, we seek to find ways in which struggles might be brought to light and documented, not simply for the sake of "multivocality," but so that the community might develop ways to deal with the problems that individuals and groups face in the academy. Rather than assuming that "new recruits" must learn to deal with their situations, we consider how the organizational culture might be changed. Unified, consensual notions of reality are rejected in favor of communities in which it is understood that different individuals and groups will always have competing concepts of reality. The challenge, of course, is to find ways to accommodate diversity and to create a climate for organizational change. In what follows, we utilize a schema offered by Cornel West that defines these challenges as intellectual, existential, and political or strategic. Through an elaboration of these points, we shall explain how they will be used in analyzing the data for the text.

The Intellectual Perspective

West has suggested that one of the key concerns in the late twentieth century "is how to think about representational practices in terms of history, culture, and society. How does one understand, analyze and enact such practices today?" (1990, 94). West's question serves as the key for this perspective and how we shall go about interpreting the data of this text. In effect, the intellectual challenge for this text is to frame our analysis so that we present the responses of the interviewees in terms of the cultural politics of difference. From this perspective, we hear divergent representations of reality as neither mistaken nor misguided, but as plausible interpretations of organizational life.

To accomplish this, it is necessary for us to locate our analysis both historically and contextually. As explained in chapter 2, to speak of promotion and tenure today is to conceive of a system that is fundamentally different from what individuals thought of as promotion and tenure at the turn of the century. Similarly, when speaking of the process today, the description varies from campus to campus. In effect, the struggle is to examine and explain the historically specific category of tenure in order to demystify and change the system to meet the needs of the twenty-first century. "Demystification tries to keep track of the complex dynamics of institutional and other related power structures," notes West, "in order to disclose options and alternatives for transformative praxis. The central role of human agency (always enacted under circumstances not of one's choosing) . . . is accented" (1990, 105). Thus, what it means to be a junior faculty member changes from generation to generation, from situation to situation. It is not enough simply to alter structures in which such individuals find themselves, but instead they must be enabled to take control of the power structures and change them. An institution is viewed in similar fashion. We regard an academic entity not simply as a repository of neutral knowledge, nor as an organization removed from society, but as an ideologically charged site at which individuals are involved in (re)creating meaning for themselves and society. One of the keys to understanding the meanings is the system of promotion and tenure, and the socializing processes involved in tenure and promotion decisions.

The Existential Perspective

This area deals with an analysis of the "cultural capital" needed to survive in academe. The French sociologist Pierre Bourdieu (1977) coined the term cultural capital to refer to the sets of linguistic and cultural competencies individuals inherit because of their class, race, and gender. Again, the point is not to suggest simplistically that those who do not have specific "competencies" ought to be equipped, for such a suggestion is inevitably doomed to failure. If we do not investigate the systems in which cultural capital is defined, then we shall be forever attempting to acculturate individuals to the mainstream rather than trying to change the system itself.

The consequences of acculturation for the individual are well known. The myth that only the "best" survive ensures that only those who conform to the norm will succeed. Individual identity is homogenized. Yet the consequences for the organizations, and particularly for educational institutions, are equally harmful. The denial of difference does not allow members of the academy, and especially students, to appreciate the diversity that exists in society now and has existed in it forever.

Such an existential dilemma has offered individuals who differ from the norm three alternatives. First, individuals can adapt, but at what cost? They may be able to navigate the promotion and tenure process, but in doing so, they all too often subjugate their own identities in order to attain success.

A second possibility is to opt out. Some individuals will not become involved in academe if the organization demands particular credentials of cultural capital. Although this is a viable option, it moves society no closer to multicultural understanding, and colleges and universities will remain islands of ethnocentricity. If this is the case, how can these institutions purport to educate the citizenry for life in the twenty-first century, when the world will be increasingly multicultural? The technological and communication transformations that we are currently experiencing will no longer allow ethnocentric isolation. If this is true, how is it possible for postsecondary organizations to remain insular and Eurocentric?

The third option is what we will promote here. Individuals and groups will retain their identities and come together in communities of difference. Dialogue will revolve around disagreement, and consensus will not be sought. The old idea of the unity of community will be abandoned in favor of academic communities that cultivate critical sensibilities and personal accountability without inhibiting individual expression (West 1990, 108).

The Strategic Perspective

We have built in this text the idea that solutions and decisions are always ideological, always philosophical. One shortcoming, however, of many proponents of critical or postmodern theories is that they critique what exists but do not propose solutions. We contend that academic institutions must take into account the intellectual and existential challenges that they face, but they then must address these challenges in the language and action of strategy.

The creation and sustenance of viable academic institutions require thoughtful reflection and action; one without the other is insufficient. The aim is consciously to redefine what we mean by terms such as "academic freedom," "tenure," "promotion," "socialization," "difference," and "community." In the economically difficult times academe has experienced in the late twentieth century, the status quo will no longer hold. For too long we have tried to effect marginal rather than fundamental change. What we propose here is a sense of possibility and potential. As in the scenario at the beginning of this chapter, the interpretation of hard-hitting reports as "bad news" that should be buried rather than acted upon is an act of strategic cowardice, not strategic vision. To continue in established patterns of behavior is not strategic because doing so will not upset the academic apple cart nor bring into question the norms with which institutions have been functioning.

But the intellectual leadership called for here requires academic *bricoleurs* who reject endless rounds of meetings, task forces, and committees that result in minuscule changes around the academic fringes yet do nothing to promote a community of difference within their institutions. We seek a more protean leadership that will bring into question who is silenced and voiceless in academe, and how we might create more democratic structures.

To call for such leadership does not mean that administrators or faculty ought to be transformed into knights errant involved in tasks worthy of an El Cid. To the contrary, the purpose of the strategic challenge is to delineate in concrete terms what critical postmodernism means for a specific institution. Accordingly, individuals need to come to terms with the history and context of ideas such as promotion and tenure, a discussion of which will be provided in the next chapter. At the same time, we do not mean to imply that simplistic recipes can be created for administrative cooks who want to solve the problems of junior faculty. The purpose of all three perspectives—intellectual, existential and political—is that each component is necessary to build a community of difference.

CHAPTER 2

Tenure as Totem and Socialization in the Academic Community

> For all of those who regard tenure as higher education's
> ultimate prize, there are at least as many who view it as
> outmoded. Tenure can be a lot like an eight-year-long the-
> atrical audition with no script and no stage direction. For
> the promise of lifetime job security, the task of tenure-
> track assistant professors generally is to wing it, to pick
> up clues from their colleagues about what would make
> them valuable assets to their department. Is it their teach-
> ing skills? The excellence of their research? The number
> of times they publish? And what about mystical factors
> such as friendship, antipathy, skill at playing academic
> power games? (Rochlin 1993)
> —(hung on a wall outside of a junior faculty office)

False Memory

Our collective memory frequently deceives us. Organizational delusion occurs in at least two forms. On one hand, members of an organization often
assume that the institutional structures and beliefs we have today have been
in place forever. On the other hand, organizational values and processes also
undergo incremental change. An individual may not notice change from day
to day, but there will be significant alterations over a generation. Participants
frequently believe, however, that the organizational standards of today are
the same as they were in the past.

Promotion and tenure exemplify both forms of institutional delusion.
Individuals frequently assume that academe always has had the structures
and processes for reward and safeguard that are in place today. We also
assume that the original reason for tenure and promotion is still valid. However, tenure is a twentieth century invention. Medieval universities had no
tenure. Harvard University, the College of William and Mary, and other co-
lonial colleges never had tenure. Institutions in the nineteenth century did
not have the system that currently is in place.

21

The rationale for the implementation of tenure at the turn of the twentieth century also differs from its purposes and effects as we prepare to enter the twenty-first century. If academe is to deal effectively with the issues surrounding junior faculty socialization, then our collective memory about promotion and tenure must be reconstructed. If postsecondary organizations operate as cultural systems, it is reasonable to investigate key terms as symbolic markers for how individuals and groups interpret reality. Accordingly, this chapter will consist of three parts. We shall first consider the historical contexts that brought about tenure, and then outline promotion and tenure scenarios at five institutions we visited. We shall conclude with a discussion of how tenure operates as a socializing process in the culture of academic organization.

Tenure in the Twentieth Century

Although no single event brought about the creation of the promotion and tenure system, it is generally agreed that it was developed as a way to guarantee *academic freedom*. The need to ensure that institutions would protect academic freedom came from two directions. A new generation of faculty had begun to explore subjects and publish ideas that differed from the accepted norms of society. Whereas in the past faculty may have accepted institutional ideologies that conformed to societal values, some new faculty did not. If their ideas varied radically from the norm, young faculty members often lost their positions.

Frequently, these new faculty had been educated in Germany, where they became accustomed to the concept of *Lehrfreiheit*. *Lehrfreiheit* upheld the "right of the university professor to freedom of inquiry and to freedom of teaching, the right to study and to report on his findings in an atmosphere of consent" (Rudolph 1962, 412). Although the concept was abstract, as Laurence Veysey has observed, it essentially pertained to management and labor issues. "Liberty," noted Veysey, "even in the academic context became inextricably linked with matters of security, status, salary, and power" (1965, 387). At the turn of the twentieth century, bureaucracy was on the rise, and the implementation of administrative structure in academe began to establish the lines of authority between faculty and administration and the board of trustees. Trouble arose when faculty members began to embrace or even discuss ideas publicly that were different from what administrators and trustees wanted to hear. The dismissal of faculty members without due process demonstrated their lack of academic freedom.

Investigators of academic freedom usually support their rhetoric with examples of individuals whose rights have been violated. Richard Ely, a liberal economist at the University of Wisconsin, came close to losing his job in 1894 because of his views (Schrecker, 1983), and Scott Nearing was fired by the University of Pennsylvania in 1915 because he opposed the use of child labor in coal mines (Slaughter 1980). Walter Metzger has written about John Mecklin, who was forced out of Lafayette College in large part because he taught about evolution (1955, 201). Professor Ollman describes the case of a political science professor, Joel Samoff, who was dismissed because he was a Marxist (1983, 46).

Most of these cases are well known, and innumerable others have occurred throughout the twentieth century. Perhaps the most celebrated case is that of Edward Ross. We repeat his story here because it illustrates how individuals in the early twentieth century confronted the abridgement of academic freedom and why they felt a system such as tenure was necessary. Indeed, Ross's story set in motion events that would refine the definition of academic freedom and result in the creation of tenure.

In 1900, Stanford University President Jordan fired the young economics professor on the grounds that his views were too liberal for the institution. Having been hired a professor in 1893, Ross had initially earned the respect and admiration of the president, the faculty, and the student body. President Jordan hired Ross from Indiana and said of him, "I do not know a man in this department in whose future I have more confidence. He shows himself entirely free from either political prejudices or the prejudices of books" (Elliott 1937, 331). Ross also thought Stanford and California were good arenas in which he could advance his career as well as his ideas. Jordan and California were "everything I could desire," (1936, 54) said Ross. Stanford was a young institution that embodied *Lehrfreiheit*, a dedication to academic excellence, and the determination to become the "Harvard of the West," as Governor Stanford had expressed his expectations to President Jordan.

From 1896 until his dismissal in 1900, Ross increasingly tested the willingness of the university to allow free discussion of ideas. President Jordan's task was to ensure that the faculty remain true to Governor Stanford's dictum that the professoriat stay clear from political activity. It is not surprising that the clash between professorial inquiry and institutional values would involve a professor of economics and sociology, insofar as the period from 1870 onward saw the central focus of intellectual inquiry in academe move away from theology and religion and toward the social and economic sciences.

By 1900, Professor Ross had embraced several controversial subjects. Among other issues, he called for the free coinage of silver and the municipal ownership of public utilities. He supported the railway union strike of 1898. He helped organize a public forum on the subject of "ruthless capitalists." He also spoke out vehemently against Asian immigration because he felt poorly paid Asian laborers took jobs away from the European-American working class. These causes were essentially socialist, overtly political, and definitely aberrant for a professor at Stanford University. The university, financed by a sole trustee, Mrs. Leland Stanford, would not stand for such attacks from one of its own faculty members. For the wife of a railroad baron who had made countless millions by employing Chinese laborers to build a privately owned railroad, Ross's words were no less than heresy. His ideas threatened the health, well-being, and stability of the entire institution, and were an insult to her dead husband and the honor of the son for whom the university had been named. The president initially supported Ross's right to speak, but gradually he came to realize the depth of Mrs. Stanford's resentment and resolve. In the final months of 1900, Mrs. Stanford demanded, and received, President Jordan's acquiescence: He would fire Edward Ross.

Ross's dismissal provoked an outcry against the Board's meddling, the impotence of a university president to defend academic freedom, and the deleterious effects the dismissal had on a dedicated professor's career and the ability to carry out intellectual inquiry. Although many of the faculty supported the president and Mrs. Stanford, seven professors resigned in protest, and many others expressed their lack of confidence in the administration. While the students kept silent, the reports of the press were shrill in condemnation: "Universal is the sentiment of reprobation of Mrs. Stanford's course," declared one. Another asserted, "No name on the faculty list has brought greater glory to the institution than Professor Ross's." (Ross 1936, 73) Ross subsequently found employment in Nebraska and eventually joined the faculty of the University of Wisconsin, where he again got himself in trouble by escorting Emma Goldman around the campus in 1910. The Wisconsin administration officially reprimanded him.

The summary dismissal of Ross and others prompted various groups to debate what academic freedom meant and how it ought to be protected. Leading intellectuals such as Charles Eliot and John Dewey weighed in with their opinions. Others such as Albion Small of the University of Chicago spoke either for or against the protection of academic freedom. The American Economics Association (AEA) became the first professional organization in the country to investigate the firing of a professor with its inquiry into the Ross case. Soon thereafter, the American Political Science Association (APSA) and the American Sociological Society (ASS) became involved in the procedural aspects of this issue.

The lack of written faculty rules and responsibilities at this time and the increasing bureaucratization of the administration of academe led to seemingly interminable conflicts, with faculty on one side and administrators and boards of trustees on the other. Different associations, such as AEA and APSA, and interested individuals finally convened a meeting of faculty that was attended by 867 professors from 60 institutions. Out of this meeting came the American Association of University Professors (AAUP). Its initial purpose was to help define "professors as professional men, not as employees" (Hofstadter and Metzger, 1955, 478). By 1915, AAUP had issued its first report on the scope and limits of academic freedom.

The authors of the report asserted that academic freedom was a fundamental principle of a college or university. The report was not so much a manifesto as a reasoned argument about rights and responsibilities of those who worked in academe. If academic freedom was the goal, then due process, tenure, and the evaluation of faculty work was the path to that goal. Although the report was predictably criticized in academic circles, this also was the document that set academe on the road to constructing the system of tenure that is in place today.

Over the next twenty-five years, AAUP's members refined their ideas. In 1940, in conjunction with the Association of American Colleges, they published a revised statement of principles pertaining to academic freedom and tenure. The document defined the terms and provided a rationale for tenure. Its statement about tenure is the basis for our current understanding of the system:

> Tenure is a means to certain ends; specifically: (1) Freedom of teaching and research and of extra-mural activities, and (2) A sufficient degree of economic security to make the profession attractive to men and women of ability. Freedom and economic security, hence tenure, are indispensable to the success of an institution in fulfilling its obligations to its students and to society. (AAUP 1985, 143)

Thus, advancing from the days when no institution had a structured tenure system, we have arrived at a time in which 85 percent of U.S. colleges and universities have some form of tenure for the protection of academic freedom. As recently as 1971, the leadership of AAUP argued that tenure "is the foundation of intellectual freedom in American colleges and universities" (Van Alstyne 1985, 149).

An additional function of tenure has been added to the protection of academic freedom. It "encourages the development of specialized learning and professional expertise by providing assurance against the dispiriting risk of summary termination" (Van Alstyne 1985, 148). Howard Bowen and Jack

Schuster have written that the system also "includes the right of faculty members to substantial autonomy in the conduct of their work" (1986, 53). Such a view defines academic freedom, then, as the unfettered freedom of inquiry into different domains of thought.

Although academic freedom retains bedrock support from faculty and administrators, other individuals often question whether tenure will provide enough protection in the twenty-first century. Recent studies of academic freedom and faculty values point out that academic freedom remains "a totem for the vast majority of respondents across disciplines and up and down the line of the institutional hierarchy" (Clark 1987, 135). For example, in one case study, for example, about faculty perceptions of academic freedom, Carol McCart observed that some respondents "felt that tenure is not an adequate protection" (1991, 245). These faculty described the changed circumstances of academe. They thought that while political threats had created the need for academic freedom, times had changed. "Pressures to secure outside funding," writes McCart, "and the growing relationship between industry and academe provide more subtle forms of research freedom constraints" (1991, 245). Respondents saw the threats to academic freedom stemming either from external sources, such as economic pressures, or from internal mandates about what is expected of faculty. Overall, most respondents in McCart's study believed that tenure provides some support for academic freedom, but others felt that the infringements tenure creates outweigh the protection it provides.

The definitions of academic freedom and tenure, then, have changed. Whereas academic freedom was once defined in universal terms of protection against political interference from external forces, individuals increasingly rely on segmented and differential definitions that reflect on their institutional, disciplinary, and individual viewpoints. Burton Clark (1987) logically points out that as the higher education system has become more diverse, individuals at different institutions view academic freedom from their respective vantage points: The researcher is concerned about research and academic freedom at the research university, the liberal arts professor defines it in terms of teaching at the liberal arts college, and so on.

The point here is not merely semantic, for if a professor must attract outside funding in order to conduct research, then we need to consider the ramifications of funding in relation to academic freedom. If a professor wishes to study topics related to gay and lesbian issues, for example, and cannot secure funding to do so, then is the individual's academic freedom being restricted? Similarly, arguments have raged on college campuses during the past decade about what is acceptable behavior in a college classroom, raising issues that the framers of academic freedom at the turn of the century never considered. Is a professor's academic freedom abridged when she is required to teach in a classroom where there is a portrait of a nude woman by Goya? Is a faculty member protected by academic freedom when he argues that Jews were the owners of the slave ships that transported Africans to the Americas, or another when he suggests that blacks are genetically inferior? If a chemistry professor decides to conduct alchemy experiments, is his freedom violated when his department officially sanctions him? All of these "real world" issues are far removed from the problems that Ross, Ely, and others faced. Nevertheless, many individuals claim that such topics legitimately fall within the domain of academic freedom.

Tenure as protection for academic freedom has also become somewhat questionable. It obviously does not protect the untenured; the increasing number of part-time, adjunct, and affiliate staff receive no support from a system that excludes them. Moreover, in McCart's study there are those who believe that tenure protects faculty to some extent but not entirely. In one respondent's words, "tenure is a good protection, but they can still get any faculty member if they want to" (1991, 243). Still others contend that "the tenure system acts against academic freedom" (1991, 240). The belief underlying these viewpoints is that either the administration will make working conditions so uncomfortable he or she will conform or resign, or that faculty will not undertake controversial projects because doing so will harm their chances for tenure and promotion.

Often individuals speak in generalities, as if "the tenure system" were the same from institution to institution. To be sure, a broad framework exists: An assistant professor enters an institution and is evaluated periodically over six years. The evaluation in the sixth year culminates with a decision to grant or deny tenure. However, the system varies tremendously from locale to locale. Thus, through an overview of five of the most common systems, we shall illustrate cultural variability across organizations. These scenarios will reveal how socialization occurs for new recruits.

The Structure of Socialization

Tenure Scenario #1

At the start of every year at a medium sized liberal arts institution a college-wide promotion and tenure committee is established. Faculty members on this committee serve staggered terms. The provost attends every meeting as a non-voting member. The Faculty Personnel Committee (FPC) meets weekly throughout the academic year. If there are numerous candidates (defined by the committee as more than six), there will be two meetings per week during the spring because the process is so time consuming.

In the sixth year, the candidate's department reaches a decision about the individual by a vote. The departmental chair then writes a letter to the FPC that outlines the candidate's perceived strengths and weaknesses. Every individual in the department also writes a letter. In addition to the letters, the committee amasses a great deal of internal information: syllabi, tests, evidence of service to the department and college and community, articles that have been published or are in progress, proceedings of conferences at which presentations were made, and student evaluations and other means of evaluating methods of teaching. Departments have different ways of collecting data about teaching. In a few departments, some faculty will periodically observe and evaluate an individual, and in others the chair will interview several students. There are departments that depend entirely on the student evaluation forms, and others that designate a single individual—usually the chair—to sit in on a few of the candidate's classes.

The candidate might solicit external letters supporting his/her research, or on occasion the committee might request a review. In general, however, few external authorities provide information that will significantly influence the decision of the committee. The committee considers candidates one at a time, and each individual's departmental chair will speak before the group about the candidate's performance. The chair also will try to answer any questions the committee may have. A recent change in the process is that the candidate also may now address the committee if he/she wishes to do so.

The committee reaches a decision without the participation of the provost, and the chair informs the president of it in a letter. The provost then confers with the president, expressing his own personal opinion. In most cases, the president will approve the decision of the committee, although there have been exceptions. The president's decision is passed on to the board of trustees, who act as a rubber stamp.

Tenure Scenario #2

At a small liberal arts college, the tenure process has been relatively casual, but it is presently undergoing change. A senior faculty member described how some time ago he found out that he had been given tenure after having taught for a few years at the college. The faculty had gotten together and voted in his favor even though he had not compiled a formal dossier. Good teaching, as determined by the informal observations of one's peers, and involvement in the life of the college were the criteria for tenure.

Now, however, a more structured process is in place. A Faculty Review and Promotion Committee (FRPC) is elected by the faculty. A candidate's department makes a recommendation to the divisional dean. The divisional dean forwards the departmental chair's letter along with his/her own assessment to the FRPC.

Every faculty member at the college has a "Career Development Plan" which outlines his/her goals and objectives over a specific period of time. This document serves as the basis for evaluating a candidate. The academic vice president has raised the standards for tenure during his term in office, so research is now somewhat important. A candidate needs to show "professional vitality" by demonstrating that he/she has attended a few conferences or perhaps published a paper or two.

Service is also important. In the tenure documents, the individual must demonstrate how he/she has worked for the betterment of the department, college, and community. The community is defined as citizens of the local towns. However, the most important criterion for tenure by far is a candidate's teaching. After observing junior faculty as they teach, senior faculty submit written evaluations. Students also provide evaluations and are interviewed by the departmental chair. Syllabi, tests, analytical instruments and other pedagogical materials are provided to the FRPC.

A candidate may submit as many as ten outside letters that evaluate his or her scholarship and teaching. These letters of support come from former students and colleagues not associated with the institution. The dean or AVP may also may solicit confidential letters. In addition to the departmental chair and divisional dean, any senior faculty member of the institution may also provide a letter about the candidate.

The committee meets in the fall to determine who is to be evaluated and what material should be requested. In the early spring, the committee meets a few times and makes a recommendation to the president. The vice president provides a separate written recommendation. The vice president and president have almost invariably supported the decision of the FRPC; the board of trustees acts as a rubber stamp.

Tenure Scenario #3

By far the most formal system we observed is at a large public research university. At the start of his/her sixth year, a candidate fills out the "rainbow files." These files consist of different colored forms that pertain to teaching, research, service, and scholarship. The review evaluation and process is multi-tiered and will take an academic year to complete.

A department makes a decision that is passed on to a division and then a college committee. The dean receives the information and recommends the candidate to a university committee that reports to the provost. The provost makes a decision, as does the president, and ultimately the board of trustees votes on the candidate. In all but the most exceptional cases, the board concurs with the recommendation of the president. The president and provost will confer on no more than a dozen cases per year in which they might overturn a decision. The most important committees and individuals in the process are in the candidate's college. The college-wide committee and the dean have the ability to halt the process by not recommending the candidate. A split or narrow vote of the committee may augur trouble at the university level.

Little attention is given to service, although a candidate for tenure is expected to show some involvement with the department and college. Information on teaching is collected, but only if an individual is charged with gross incompetence will it be used as a means to deny tenure. Faculty members from the candidate's department will write an analysis of an individual's teaching after one or two observations. The evaluators also may have scanned syllabi or test materials, but the actual materials are not included in the rainbow files. Student evaluations based on a standardized form are included and are next in importance to the evaluation of teaching.

Unquestionably the most important area of evaluation involves research and scholarship. All the candidate's articles and presentations are put into the dossier, along with evaluations from outside reviewers. Perhaps more than any other source of information, the various committees rely on external letters from reviewers who are affiliated with institutions that are comparable to the candidate's. These letters comment exclusively on the individual's ability as a researcher and scholar.

There are no formal interviews of department chairs or candidates. If a problem occurs or there are questions at the university level, then it is conceivable that the candidate's dean and one other faculty member who is knowledgeable about the individual would be requested to appear before the committee in the spring. The committees work according to a specific timetable, with the departmental ones meeting in early fall, and the provost and president concluding their work in late spring. Each committee generally meets no more than three or four times a year. The board meets in May, after which letters are sent to the candidates informing them whether tenure has been conferred or denied.

Tenure Scenario #4

At a smaller research-oriented public university, the process is less formal and time consuming, but research remains the most important aspect in a candidate's file. A candidate compiles a dossier that includes a resume, articles, a summary of teaching scores, and outside letters. The departmental faculty receive the file in December, along with other confidential letters that have been solicited by the departmental chair or divisional director.

In January, tenured faculty of the department vote, and the chair then passes their decision on to the Vice President for Academic Affairs (VPAA) along with his/her own written evaluation. The VPAA convenes a meeting of all the departmental chairs in February. In the course of one long evening, the individuals discuss the strengths and weaknesses of each candidate, after which they vote by secret ballot. There is no college-wide committee. The VPAA sends the scores of the vote and his/her own recommendation to the president. In the recent past, the president and board have not become seriously involved in reviewing the decisions of the VPAA.

Because of the professional nature of the institution, service is generally defined as off-campus work related to one's area of specialization. College-wide committee work is not considered particularly important, but conducting a workshop, serving as a consultant, or providing technical assistance to other members of one's profession is viewed favorably. With regard to the evaluation of teaching, the institution has a hundred-item questionnaire that all students are asked to complete at the end of each course. One question pertains to how the course in question compares with others that the student has taken. The institutional norm is 2.8, so candidates generally need to demonstrate that their teaching is at or above the norm.

Although teaching is taken somewhat seriously, by far the most important aspect of a candidate's file is the ability to conduct funded research. Faculty members are expected to publish at least one or two articles per year in refereed journals, and they need to obtain outside grants and contracts to support their research. Individuals commented that if a typical candidate had not obtained outside funding, then he/she would probably not be granted tenure. The faculty, department chairs, and VPAA are the primary arbiters of quality, and outside letters are significantly less important.

Tenure Scenario #5

At a medium-sized private university, the criteria used to evaluate a candidate vary from college to college although the processes are the same. At one college, the applicants who visit the campus are told that they probably will not get tenure because research is so important, and at another college teaching is stressed. Service is unimportant at all colleges, although one must demonstrate involvement to some extent; again, the form depends upon the college. A professional school expects service to the profession, and the humanities and liberal arts view service as departmental and college-wide committee work.

The process is three-tiered. A candidate's department passes initial judgment, and the departmental chair must write a letter with which all faculty concur. The letter then goes to a college-wide committee that determines by secret ballot the worth of the candidate's dossier. Each committee member also submits his/her appraisal to the dean. The dean then writes an evaluation and passes it to the provost. There is no university-wide committee. The provost makes a separate recommendation to the president. In only rare cases is the president or board involved.

The college requires outside letters of support and evidence of scholarship and research. All works in progress and published materials are submitted. The college is particularly concerned with the prestige of the presses and journals that have published the books and articles. A list of service activities and presentations is also required. The committees use teaching evaluations and departmental observations as well as letters from former students to assess pedagogy.

Our purpose in presenting these scenarios has been twofold. First, it is important to indicate the variations in internal processes that institutions employ. As the following chapters will show, academic administrators often speak as if there were only one best system, and consequently, they act as if any deviation will in some way damage the process and outcome. The comparative perspective outlined here reveals the diversity that exists.

Second, we have sought to portray systems as they actually exist without commenting on their individual strengths or weaknesses. In the next chapter, we shall present individuals' interpretations of these systems to depict in greater detail the dynamic cultures in which they exist. The point, then, is first to consider the diverse structures within academe and then to analyze how individuals interpret these structures and act within them. Before doing so, however, we shall discuss specific individuals who are involved in the tenure process and then analyze this information from the aspect of socialization.

Actors in the Process

Structurally, in addition to the protagonist's role of the candidate, there are four key actors involved in the tenure process. To be sure, an individual faculty member, a university administrator, or a member of the community may play a role in someone's candidacy; in general, however, (1) the departmental chair, (2) the dean and/or provost, (3) the president and board of trustees, and (4) the external reviewers are the principle players.

In many respects, the department chair plays a curious role. As we have seen, in some instances the chair serves as a go-between for the candidate and various committees. In this sense, the chair is more coach and confidant than evaluator. At the same time, the chair is often the one who evaluates a candidate's teaching and expresses his/her opinion to the committees at large, which in turn, will use this information to reach their decision. The chair may also act as the recorder for the department and pass along verbal and written judgments of the individual.

Another odd aspect of the departmental chair's role is that unlike other structural personnel such as the dean or provost, the chair may be involved in a tenure case only periodically. Small departments or those with a high concentration of tenured faculty, may have an assistant professor come up for tenure only once in a decade. Surely, the formal and informal skills associated with the process must vary with the degree to which an individual is involved. In many respects, it appears that no other individual plays so important a role as the department chair, and yet, no one else has such ambiguous or periodic responsibilities. The chair's role is often ill-defined and may vary within an institution. Over time, a chair may come to understand the intricacies of the process through systematic involvement, or he/she may never be involved in a decisive way. As the convener of departmental meetings, the chair is formally important to the candidate; but as someone who is often asked to speak on the candidate's behalf or provide advice to the individual, the chair's informal relationship with the individual is critical.

The dean's and provost's roles are more formal and evaluative. These individuals in general have no vote in committees and leave initial decisions to the faculty. However, as we have indicated a dean or provost often sits in on committees, and in one case the vice president convened the committee that voted on the candidate's tenure. When an individual serves on a committee permanently, even in a non-voting capacity, and other members come and go by election, then the permanent member can accrue a great deal of power by serving as the memory of the body. Similarly, when an individual convenes and chairs the committee that will vote on a candidate, the person is equally important.

We have also mentioned the various ways in which vice presidents and deans are involved in the process administratively. In some cases, these individuals have no formal role, and in others they are one rung on a multi-runged system. In one scenario, the vice president had the final say as to who received tenure, and in another the individual served as an informal advisor to the president. In all cases, unlike the departmental chair, these individuals are involved in the tenure process on a yearly basis. In fact, in many instances, this is one of the key aspects of their work.

The president and board of trustees are also involved in this process every year. In a few instances, the board played an active role, but in most cases, the trustees were passive observers who merely confirmed what others had decided. The presidential role differed from institution to institution. Some presidents saw themselves as being actively involved in confirming or overruling decisions, and others played no role at all. However, by the time the candidate's portfolio arrived on the president's desk, the individual's fate was sealed. Even in situations where the president became involved in the process, he/she made decisions about fewer than ten percent of the candidates. As we shall discuss in the next chapter, however, perhaps more important than the president's being actively involved in a tenure decision is the symbolic tone that was set about institutional priorities pertaining to promotion and tenure.

The final role that should be mentioned is that of the external reviewer. In some cases, the institution did not consider any outside letters of recommendation, and in others, these letters were the most important documents in a candidate's dossier. Most external reviewers comment on two facets of a candidate's record: research and scholarship. A few institutions solicited letters from former students who were considered qualified to judge a candidate's teaching, but most reviewers were senior faculty in the candidate's discipline at other institutions.

The candidates often requested that individuals write letters on their behalf, or they gave the names of potential reviewers to their departmental chair. Some department chairs also compiled their own list of referees in order to ensure impartiality. These letters usually ranged from one to four pages and were based on a review of a candidate's articles. In some instances the institution paid the reviewers, but this was generally not the case. Some reviewers received nothing more than the candidate's curriculum vitae on which to comment, and other institutions provided the reviewers with a sample of the candidate's writing.

Comparing the Structures

It is apparent that institutions use vastly different processes in their efforts to ensure tenure. One should not be surprised, perhaps, that a large university is more concerned with publications while a small liberal arts college pays more attention to teaching. What is curious is the different ways in which evaluations are structured.

Some institutions use outside evaluators while others do not. At one college, a committee meets every week for a year, and at another there is only one evening meeting. One institution has multi-levels of review, and another has no all-institution committee. Why is there such disparity? Why does one group of faculty members feel the need to pore over a candidate's files for the better part of a year, and another group believe they are able to make an informed decision in an evening? Why do some academics presume they are capable of making informed judgments about an individual's research even if it is not in their domain, while other scholars feel compelled to seek advice from experts whom they do not know?

Similarly, some institutions rely more heavily on administrative decisions while others place the responsibility for decision-making in the hands of the faculty. At one institution, teaching is evaluated by having a senior faculty member observe a class, and at another institution, a student questionnaire is deemed to provide sufficient information with which to make an informed decision. Virtually all institutions discount the importance of service, but all institutions retain service as an evaluative category. If one were to contemplate the structure of tenure as if it were a purely rational process (which it is not), one would ask why service remains a category if it is meaningless? Is it not paradoxical that in virtually all areas of the institution, the student voice has no influence, yet the collective judgment of the student body about the quality of a teacher's classes is often given the most serious consideration in the tenure process? Conversely, on what basis do institutions contend that the observation of a class or two by a senior professor constitutes a fair or systematic evaluation of teaching? None of the institutions we visited had developed standardized observation forms, so the decision about what to evaluate was left entirely to the discretion of the reviewer.

Throughout the twentieth century, academe has developed and refined what we referred to earlier as a central "totem"—academic freedom (Clark 1987). In order to protect this totem, institutions created their own cultural system—tenure. The structure of tenure is culturally based within an organization and pertains not merely to what is important to its participants— research versus teaching—but also to how the participants decide whether an initiate is worthy of receiving the totem. When we analyze the structure of tenure, we find cultural paradoxes: Teaching is important, but we allow individuals who are not considered important in other domains to make decisions; a biologist feels competent to evaluate an archaeologist's scholarship; a committee decides that one evening is sufficient time to reach a decision that potentially will cost the institution millions of dollars if the individual granted tenure stays until retirement; another committee decides to peruse all the syllabi of a candidate, and so on.

Perhaps the greatest cultural anomaly is that this system was devised to protect academic freedom, yet no consideration has been given to how it affects pre-tenure candidates, in terms of socializing them to the nature of inquiry and the meaning of community. According to the rules of the system, once individuals have proven their worth, they are then granted academic freedom; but until that time, we need never consider whether their freedom is abridged or denied. Is it not a bizarre structure of socialization we have constructed where the ultimate goal—academic freedom—is never taken into consideration as candidates are considered on the basis of their teaching, research, service and scholarship?

Socialization and Academic Community

If we are to use critical postmodernism as a lens through which to analyze the representational practices of academic freedom and tenure in these institutions, what might we see? One immediate point is that in the institutions we visited, the subject of academic freedom is rarely mentioned in discussions of the tenure system. Instead, the main concern is usually what different attributes should be considered in judging a particular candidate. The balance between one's research and teaching is a common topic. The impact of committee work on academic freedom is sometimes questioned. It is ironic that the tenure system came into being partly as a result of the problems of Edward Ross, but if tenure had been in place during his time at Stanford, he probably would not have been protected. His speeches and writing would have derailed him from his tenure-track.

Is the structure in place socializing individuals to particular norms, or is it promoting "options and alternatives for transformative praxis," as Cornel West noted in chapter 1? The structure seems designed to filter candidates rather than to advance diverse concepts of inquiry. The cultural system of organizations offering tenure provide diverse ways of evaluating individuals, but it does not seem to socialize them to survive and thrive in a community based on difference.

Robert Merton (1957) thought of socialization in general as a means to achieve group solidarity. From a neo-Marxian perspective, Pierre Bourdieu has written that socialization is a means of reproducing the cultural capital of society (1977). Our interpretation of faculty socialization differs from the more traditional notions of Merton and Bourdieu. Interestingly, although they critique socialization from very different theoretical perspectives— structural-functionalism and Marxism—both assume socialization to be a process whereby the organization shapes the individual. We view socialization as a ritualized process that involves the transmission of the organizational culture. Tenure is the strongest example of a socializing mechanism for new faculty in that it involves the exchange and definition of thought and action.

From a critical postmodern perspective from which we are trying to develop the idea of communities of difference, we are suggesting that participants in an institution of higher education need to reconsider how faculty become enmeshed within the organizational setting. Instead of a unidirectional process in which individuals must adapt to organizational norms, we intend to develop a bidirectional scheme of socialization. Individuals should be encouraged to influence and change the organization, just as the organizational mores may influence and change them. Our point here is that as an interpretive site of negotiation, the culture of an organization has the potential to be changed in a number of different ways if the participants within it are allowed to express their diversity. Socialization is a highly charged process through which different individuals and groups come together to determine organizational beliefs and attitudes. Thus, rather than treating tenure as an abstract system for safeguarding conceivably outmoded concepts of academic freedom, we need to think of it as a cultural process that orients individuals and the organization to evolving institutional values and ideologies.

In the next chapters, we shall discuss socialization as a two-stage process. *Anticipatory socialization* takes place before an individual sets foot on campus. They are socialized in this sense as graduate students, or as faculty at other institutions (Tierney and Rhoads 1993). For our purposes, however, we shall consider more fully the second stage: *organizational socialization*. This occurs first through what we call *initial entry* and then by *role continuance*. We contend that thinking of tenure and junior faculty life in this manner is as important for protecting academic freedom as were the initial efforts to establish the tenure system at the turn of the century. Simply stated, a structure cannot ultimately be the arbiter and protector of an ideal; people define, interpret, and implement structures and policies. From a cultural perspective, comprehension of the ongoing processes of socialization is necessary if we wish to develop more inclusive communities that give individuals the freedom to challenge ideas.

We define "initial entry" as those acts that take place prior to entering the organization and immediately thereafter. The manner in which an individual is interviewed for a job and the kind of orientation that occurs are examples of socializing acts in this phase. "Role continuance" takes place throughout the tenure process. Socialization in this phase is both formal and informal. The tenure process itself is formal, whereas the casual conversations that individuals have on this and other subjects are examples of informal socializing experiences.

Dimensions of Organizational Socialization

Socializing experiences such as tenure can be broken apart into discrete activities. In what follows, we shall delineate the six dimensions of socialization within organizations (Van Maanen and Schein, 1979). In succeeding chapters, we shall discuss these dimensions in greater detail and describe their impact on the individuals we interviewed. One caveat is important: Van Maanen and Schein do not mean to suggest that one dimensional form is better than another and neither do we. One must first comprehend the schema and then analyze how it operates in different organizational cultures.

1. Collective vs. Individual

Collective socialization occurs when a similar group of individuals undergo common experiences. New graduate students who must take common examinations or soldiers in boot camp are examples of groups that undergo collective socialization. New faculty may experience collective socialization if there are significant numbers of them working in a culture that is cohesive and unitary. Distinctive colleges such as Reed or Swarthmore are examples of cohesive cultures, and large urban commuter institutions are the opposite.

Individual socialization occurs when individuals are processed in singular fashion. By and large, tenure-track faculty participate in individual socialization. Institution-wide activities usually do not take place, and faculty are isolated within their departments. The department rather than the college or institution becomes the locus of identity. Within the department there may be at most only one or two new faculty members every year, and the vast majority of socializing experiences occur within the domain of the department.

2. Formal vs. Informal

We noted earlier that socialization occurs in formal and informal manners. In formal socialization, the recruits are separated from the rest of the organization in order to participate in a series of activities designed specifically for them. Orientation sessions on college campuses and year-end reviews are perhaps the best examples of formal mechanisms of socialization.

Informal socialization is casual. Who speaks with whom around the water cooler, for example, or the kinds of after-work activities that take place are informal in nature and typify this kind of socialization. We shall give particular attention to this dimension of socialization as it occurs with regard to women faculty and faculty of color. Individuals who differ from the norm often find stark differences in informal interactions with their colleagues as opposed to interactions that take place in formal settings. That is to say, in a formal socializing experience all individuals participate in like manner. However, junior faculty women in science, for example, often feel that they have fewer opportunities to become involved in cooperative efforts with their senior male colleagues than their male peers do. In large part this is due to the informal way in which research is structured.

3. Random vs. Sequential

Random socialization occurs when activities leading to a particular goal are not clearly delineated. Conversely, in sequential socialization, specific steps are identified for new personnel to follow as they advance in the organization. This dimension of socialization is more ordered and comprehensible, and it has logical ties with the two prior dimensional aspects of formal and collective practices.

Random socialization probably best describes the tenure process. Although the goal is clear—to achieve tenure—the process one should follow to achieve this goal is ambiguous. How many articles does one need to write, for example? How important is teaching in the evaluation of a candidate? Or what is to be evaluated? None of this is ever particularly clear. Sequential socialization may be seen in large bureaucracies where qualifications and requirements for promotion at a higher level are spelled out in elaborate detail.

4. Fixed vs. Variable

This dimension is temporal in nature. Is there a specified timetable for socialization or is it random? Schooling is a good example of both forms. A student typically graduates from high school in four years. A graduate student, however, will take an unspecified amount of time to complete the requirements for a doctorate. For junior faculty, the tenure process is in general a fixed dimension; at the end of six years, they either obtain it or it is denied. To be sure, some faculty are allowed or encouraged to apply for tenure before the sixth year, and some institutions permit faculty to stop the "tenure clock" if they have had a child, an illness or an accident.

5. Serial vs. Disjunctive

This is the dimension that pertains to role models and mentors. Serial socialization occurs when a new faculty has an experienced member of the organization to serve as a guide. In disjunctive socialization, there are no organizational role models for the newcomer. Obviously, new faculty may find themselves in either of these situations. Some will be assigned a senior mentor, or a department chair may assume the responsibility for orienting the

Fig. 1
Faculty Socialization

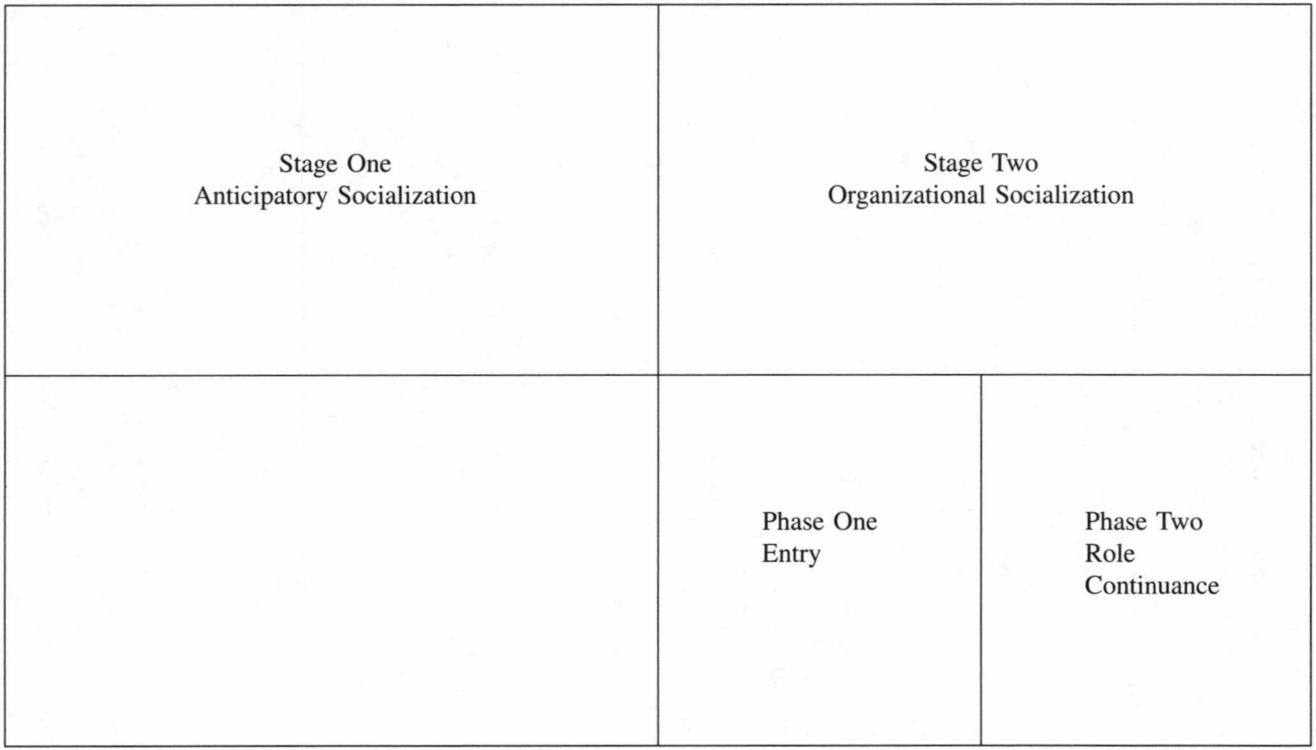

Stage One
Anticipatory Socialization

Stage Two
Organizational Socialization

Phase One
Entry

Phase Two
Role
Continuance

Fig. 2
Dimensions of Faculty Socialization

1. Collective .... Individual
   (group)   vs.   (singular)

2. Formal .... Informal
   (isolated from organizational members)   vs.   (interwoven w/ organizational members)

3. Random .... Sequential
   (unclear and ambiguous)   vs.   (ordered steps)

4. Fixed .... Variable
   (specific timetable)   vs.   (no timetable)

5. Serial .... Disjunctive
   (lead by role models)   vs.   (no role models)

6. Investiture .... Divestiture
   (affirming individual charac.) vs.   (transforming individual charac.)

Adapted from Tierney & Rhoads (1993).

new individual. Other junior faculty will "go it alone" and not have anyone in particular to turn to for guidance.

In some institutions, serial socialization occurs by design, but most often we have found that it is haphazard. A senior faculty member may offer assistance of his/her own volition because it seems necessary or the right thing to do, but there are no organizational reward structures to encourage this. We should also note that unlike the other dimensions, this is an area where the new faculty members also have a choice. Not everyone wants or needs a mentor. Some junior faculty consciously forego serial socialization and seek help from individuals outside the institution, such as members of their dissertation committee or former classmates from graduate school.

6. Investiture vs. Divestiture

This final dimension pertains to experiences that either affirm or transform a new faculty member's perceptions, attitudes, and beliefs. Investiture refers to activities that confirm what an individual learned about faculty life in graduate school. Divestiture occurs when an newcomer must change in order to adapt to the culture of the organization.

For example, a new faculty member who attended a research university may experience a radically different life if he/she is employed by a community college. The anticipatory socialization experiences that took place in graduate school may have led the individual to believe that faculty work always involves research, whereas at a less prestigious institution, opportunities for research may be few and far between. As will be discussed in chapter 4, it is also possible that those individuals who differ from the norm—women and people of color—also may experience divestiture if they feel compelled to conform to values that are not their own.

A brief review is in order. We began this chapter by outlining how tenure was developed to protect academic freedom. We then discussed various approaches to tenure to indicate the dramatically different ways in which the system is interpreted depending on organizational culture. We raised questions about how tenure protects academic freedom and suggested that because tenure exists within a cultural framework, it should be considered a central act of socialization. We then described how we shall use critical postmodernism to analyze the socialization of junior faculty, and we discussed the dimensions of socialization. Each dimension provides ways to understand the socialization of junior faculty in the tenure process. We shall now turn to data derived from two years of interviews to determine how these dimensions of socialization are enacted and interpreted by the participants, and how these various structures of tenure influence the development of new faculty.

CHAPTER 3

The Tenure and Promotion Years

Initiation

An assistant professor recalled his job interview and arrival on campus:

> I was met at the plane by the department chair and another older faculty member. They took me to the chair's house where we had a scotch, which I thought was a bit too quick. I don't drink much to begin with, and after a plane trip I felt woozy. Later that week we had dinner at [a local restaurant], and there was a party for secretaries going on. The department chair kept making sexist jokes about the different women all through dinner. "Check her out," he'd say, or "wow, she's stacked." It was very uncomfortable. I didn't know what to do, how to act.
>
> It was the best and only real job offer I had, so I accepted. When I arrived, however, they didn't have an office for me, so they stuck me in a senior faculty member's office who was on sabbatical. When he returned, he was really pissed off at me, but I didn't have anything to do with it. I was also assigned to teach what we had explicitly said I wouldn't teach.
>
> The weirdest thing was my moving expenses. When I got here, the chair told me that he couldn't pay moving, although he said he could when I accepted the job. Instead, he told me to fake a trip to a conference, fill out the forms, he'd sign them, and I'd get reimbursed. So here I was, my first semester on campus without an office, told to teach a class that I was unprepared for, and given forms to fill out that made me lie. Like anybody in my shoes, I was just out of graduate school and broke. It just wasn't a good way to start.

To be sure, this faculty member's initiation into the culture of his department, campus, and profession is an exception to the rule. This was the only instance we heard of in which a department chair asked a faculty member to do something unethical—submit a fraudulent reimbursement form. We did hear, however, from faculty who had had to teach a course that they were not assigned, or arrived on campus to discover that they did not have an office or a laboratory or a graduate assistant when they had been told there would be no problem. Other faculty who had not thought to ask about specific kinds of support arrived on campus to discover that their colleagues had computers but they did not, or their office mates had secured funding to attend a conference but there was none left for them, or the salary had been negotiable and someone with the same credentials had struck a better bargain.

This chapter extends these observations by using the framework developed in chapters 1 and 2 to analyze the data for this study. We shall offer a broad analysis of what it means to be a junior faculty member, and in the following two chapters, we shall focus specifically on issues that pertain to women and people of color. We shall begin our discussion of anticipatory socialization by elaborating on other faculty members' recollections of their interviews and arrival on their respective campuses. Then we shall discuss formal and informal mentoring. In the third part of the chapter, we shall analyze faculty work—teaching, research, and service; in the final section, we shall discuss the ritual year during which the candidate compiles and presents his or her dossier and the faculty votes for or against tenure.

Anticipatory Socialization

Job Interviews

Across institutional type and discipline, virtually all of the candidates gave one of four reasons for having accepted employment at their respective institutions: (a) it was the only job they were offered; (b) it was the kind of community they wanted for either their partner or their children; or (c) their department or institution had a particular characteristic that they were seeking; or (d) they were following a partner who had relocated. Given the hiring climate of the 1980s and 1990s, it is not surprising that by far the most common response was that they accepted the job because no other offers were forthcoming, or they decided to take a firm offer rather than waiting to see whether something better might turn up.

"I applied for about 60 jobs, got three interviews, and this was the only one that offered me a tenure-track position. Of course I took it," explained one individual. "I wanted a job almost anywhere, and I applied for almost whatever I saw. There were a few exceptions, but I ended up taking what came to me," said a second person. A third person concurred: "They had said that the job market would be better, but it sure wasn't in English. There are horror stories out there, and I'm just glad I got a position in a good school." Another said, "I applied to about one hundred jobs and of all the programs in the country; if I could have written a job description for myself this would have been it."

Some individuals were grateful for having obtained employment in a major city where it might be easier for their partner to find work, or in a community with good schools. As one individual explained, "I might have had a job offer in New York City, but with two young kids, I never really thought about it. The schools. In fact I didn't apply for any major city. It was a big consideration." A second person had similar misgivings about big cities, but applied anyway and ultimately ended up in a mid-sized city: "My wife works as an accountant in a business firm, and when we did this, we were sure we didn't want a commuter marriage. So jobs out in the boon-docks were avoided. I also wasn't wild about metropolitan life, but I applied wherever I thought I had a shot and my wife might be able to get a job. This has been a good compromise." A third person had a different perspective on rural life: "As a gay man, I just didn't want the loneliness and isolation of small-town living. If I'd had a partner, it would have been different, but I went to grad school in a rural area, and I had had enough." A man who was paralyzed said that "one of the most important aspects of [his] decision was that this particular university had access for a wheelchair and [he] could get in and out of almost everywhere."

About a quarter of those interviewed had some idea about the kind of professional life they wanted. Their decision about where to apply was inevitably influenced, positively or negatively, by the research programs they had observed in graduate school. "I had no desire," said one person, "to get into the rat race that I saw in my department." Another person agreed, "I like to do research, but I did not apply to any research universities because the professors I worked with really didn't have a life. And the politics were incredible." A third person added, "I didn't want the pressure. Writing my dissertation was okay, but I also knew I'd never make it for tenure if I had to publish all the time."

On the other hand, some individuals made explicit decisions to seek out research universities:

> I'm good at research and I like it. My advisor encouraged me to apply to a research school, and this department is the best in the country. They have the resources for me to start up a lab and to have a graduate student [assistant]. That's important for a research program. I'm happy here. I probably spend thirty percent of my time writing grants, thirty percent of my time in the lab and doing research, thirty percent teaching, and another thirty percent on service and department stuff. Yeah, I know. I'm busy! I knew it would be like this.

Although this individual knew what to expect when she consciously chose a research university, others did not. As we shall see, what they discovered did not always come as a pleasant surprise. Basically, the norm for potential faculty members seeking employment is to apply for any open position regardless of institutional type. A history professor obviously knew there was a difference between a major public research university and a small private institution, but in a tight job market one applies for whatever is available. Similarly, in the sciences, a candidate in physics saw no alternative to applying for work in all types of institutions. At one small liberal arts college we visited, the physics department had received over 150 applications for one position.

A few professors chose their institution based on shared intellectual and political interests. A Latina in a financially strapped urban university said, "I wanted to be in a public university with progressive faculty" and a Latino at a private university said, "I valued what the college was trying to do in terms of its commitment to social issues—to issues of social justice, to issues of women, and to issues of minorities."

Although the faculty workload varies from institution to institution, the job interview is essentially the same, regardless of whether it is a rural comprehensive state university, a selective private liberal arts college, or an urban public institution. No interviewee was on campus for less than one day or more than two days. Some came to the campus over the weekend to get an idea of what the housing or schools were like. The candidates spent an intensive period in one-on-one interviews with individual faculty. The dean or an associate dean generally met with them, although the meetings seemed perfunctory. Fewer than ten percent of the applicants were asked to teach a class or interact with students in any formal manner, but the majority had to give a presentation based on research. One individual remembers the interview as follows:

> It was a blur. They kept me so busy I was not able to get nervous. I don't know what advice I'd give about changing it. It's just a gamut that you run through and if they like you for some inexplicable reason you get chosen. It's not scientific at all. It comes down to personal chemistry between you and the senior faculty.

Data from the interviews overwhelmingly support what this individual said, with a few caveats. "You have to give a good presentation, make them know you know your field," said one person. "Three people showed up for my seminar, so I don't know how that counted, but I think I seemed acceptable in a non-controversial way," commented one junior faculty member. Another person said, "I'm using feminist theory, and for this department that's still suspect, but I know the traditional methods and canon, so they were appeased—initially." An individual in the sciences who ended up at a research university went one step further: "You have to have a research agenda, be grant active, and assure them that you will hit the ground running. They're right, too, because if you don't, you're sunk." A fourth person offered an interesting insight on the need to have an active research agenda and how the faculty discovered whether the candidate had one:

We have two big presentations here. One is where you present your research. But in the first day you are asked to give an "informal talk" where you are expected to discuss your research agenda, what you'd do if you came here. I didn't know it at the time, but I've seen searches occur since then, and at the end of the hour everyone knows if you'll be offered the job. It gives the faculty a chance to hear what you will do, and more than anything else, it makes or breaks you.

A professor from a large research university described her lack of preparedness to interview at a small liberal arts college: "My major professor hadn't prepared me for interviewing at smaller institutions. . . . I didn't know that meetings with particular people had any relevance. . . . I kind of blew off meetings with students, I didn't even know their opinion counted." And a man described the pre-screening process that goes on at national conferences: "I went to the national meeting in New Orleans and had twenty-one interviews in two days."

Formal meetings about the responsibilities of the job might have taken place with the departmental chair or the dean, but usually discussions were quite general. "The dean kept me waiting for forty-five minutes, and when I finally did meet him, it was just pleasantry," recalled one person. A second individual said, "I had lots of questions that I wanted answered, but I was never sure when the appropriate time was, or whom to ask. If you can believe this, I ended up speaking with the graduate students." On the other hand, one person said, "The department chair had me over for a glass of wine with his wife the afternoon before everything started. He clued me in on what to expect, what I would be doing, and the specifics of the job. I appreciated his forthrightness." One person said of his dean, however, "It was clear he didn't know who I was, that he was just going through the motions. He still wouldn't know me if he walked in here right now."

Brief mention should be made of certain points that we shall discuss in greater detail in the final chapter. When we speak of anticipatory socialization, we are referring to the kinds of socializing experiences a candidate has before arriving on campus to assume a position. When a dean does not take the time to meet with an applicant, that sends one message, and when a dean attends an individual's presentation, that sends another. We also found it interesting that even at institutions where teaching is considered more important than research, candidates were either rarely asked to teach a class, or students were virtually excluded from the interview process. What kind of message about faculty-student relationships is sent to a candidate if students play no part at all in the interview? Similarly, if most individuals remember their initial experience on campus as little more than a blur or a form of initiation hazing in which one is made to run a gamut, one wonders how a more positive situation might be developed in which interviewees gain a sense of the mission and values of the institution. To be sure, the interview process will always be an ambiguous and nerve-wracking experience for the interviewee, but is it possible to develop a schema that is not as haphazard as what occurs now?

Arrival on Campus

There was tremendous variation in when and from whom an individual received an offer. The one who reported that his department had an "informal talk" said, "At the end of the talk the chair of the search committee told me he thought they would offer me the job. They called me the day after I arrived home." Another person had the opposite experience. His interview had taken place in the late fall: "I didn't hear anything from anyone. I waited and figured I'd lost the job. I was just about to accept a one year appointment where I was a grad student in the summer when the department chair called and asked if I was still interested in the position." A third person had a typical experience: "I guess they called me about a month after the interview and offered me the job."

Either the departmental chair, the chair of the search committee, or the dean of the college made the job offers. The offers were usually straightforward, but how much the candidate knew about what to ask for varied tremendously. A man said, "I didn't know enough to ask questions when I was interviewing. . . . I didn't know how to bargain or ask for more . . . there aren't many jobs in English so in a strange way you feel grateful that people want to hire you and you don't want to ask for more." "I was so glad to get an offer I just said yes right away, and that was it," said another person; "I should have asked for a computer because I didn't get it until my second year." A third person was a bit less hesitant, but still had no idea how to discuss matters such as salary: "The department chair had asked me if there was anything I thought I would need, and I had made sure that all faculty offices had a computer, so I said I'd like one. He said it could be arranged. We never discussed salary. I grew up in a family where it's gauche to bargain, a big faux pas, so I had neither the inclination or realization that I should have. I should have." A fourth person concurred: "One thing graduate students should learn is what to ask for. The only time I ever bargained for anything was when I bought a car, and I couldn't believe that here I was applying for a faculty position and I was expected to barter."

Faculty in the sciences and engineering usually had a much clearer notion of what they needed; indeed, negotiations frequently began while the candidate was on campus so the applicant had some sense of what was available. As one person recalled, "I was told even before I came for the interview that if I were hired, they would give me $50,000 to start my lab. It was very clear. No bargaining." Another person added, "They knew in hiring me that they would need to buy expensive equipment for my lab. It came to about $250,000, and I didn't have to bargain, I wasn't expected to, because they never would have hired me to do my work if they couldn't come up with the funds necessary to start a lab." However, some individuals had not gotten clear messages. "I arrived and found out that another junior professor had asked for a grad assistant and gotten one. That burned me. Of course I needed one, but just because I didn't know the rules, I got screwed."

Between the time individuals were offered a job and when they arrived on campus, there was little if any, communication. "I had questions about my teaching, about where to order books, things like that," said one person, "but I didn't want to seem like a typical woman who asks lots of dumb questions, so I never called anybody." A second person learned not to ask questions the hard way: "About a month after I was offered the job, I thought I'd give our chair a call and ask if he could send me some sample syllabi, maybe give me a hint about how to go about looking for housing. I felt stupid when I called. Sort of like I had disturbed him. Sort of like the college freshman with the beanie. So I just waited until I arrived and could talk to other junior faculty." Other individuals had better experiences. "They assign you a mentor here," explained one person, "and he called a couple of times throughout the summer to see how he could help." Another person also received a warmer welcome: "My department is very friendly. The department chair arranged for me to come back and look for housing, and he had a group of faculty over for dinner to his house. It was nice, so different from the interview!" A brand new professor said of her chair, "We talked constantly, from the time he hired me. . . . He sent me syllabi and I could ask him questions about what kind of courses to prepare."

When individuals arrived on campus, their experiences were similarly diverse: "The college has a faculty group who actually help you unload your stuff. I couldn't believe it, and it was incredibly helpful," said one person. "As soon as I got into town," said another individual, "my department chair had demanded that I let her know. So I called and she went out of her way to help me the first few weeks in getting oriented." Not everyone fared as well. One individual said, "I was totally on my own. Me and my map figuring out where everything was." Another person said, "I'm used to doing things my way and that's lucky because no one was here to help."

The experience of beginning work also varied from person to person: "The secretary gave me my office key and teaching schedule. It was no big deal as far as I can remember," recalled one individual. Another person said, "They were supposed to have ordered a computer for me, but when I arrived the computer was there but I didn't have a keyboard or printer. That came second semester." A third person had a similar experience: "To do my work, I need a particular kind of equipment for the lab, but they had trouble ordering it, so I didn't get it until the latter half of the first year. That really slowed me up." Some individuals also discovered they had received an impossible teaching schedule:

> Usually they give new faculty a light load the first semester, but someone had taken a leave of absence at the last minute and they assigned one of his classes to me. Then another person had an accident and they switched his courses around and I ended up teaching a class I was totally unprepared for. I felt I never stopped running the entire first year.

The perception of what orientation, if any, was available for new faculty members varied depending on the position of the individual in an organization. A dean, for example, said, "We have implemented a very clear, very straightforward orientation for new faculty that I participate in. It's when I meet them." An individual in his college said, "It's a joke, really. Filling out forms and telling you what to do and what not to do." A second person in the college said, "You could call it an orientation, yes. But it's not what you mean. It's more a bureaucratic thing." At another institution, an individual recalled, "What I remember is discussing stuff like if you should keep your promotion and tenure files in a notebook or a box. I couldn't believe it."

Departmental chairs also felt that they provided an orientation: "I speak with all new faculty when they arrive," said one chair, "and I help them get started." Yet an assistant professor in the department remembered, "He's a busy man and he kept saying that first semester that we should get together, but we never did. It was fine. I learned things on my own by asking other junior faculty." The chair of a large department in a research university started a retreat for junior faculty to, as he put it, "create some bonding and let them get acquainted with one another's work and talk about their own concerns." The chair of another large department said, "I promote my role as the observing uncle, the facilitator, the helper. . . . I talk to them [new faculty] about their background, immediate plans, research, teaching, and so on. I tell them about the opportunities in this department and the resources that are available to them." For the chair this talk is important because "it gives me a sense of their general plan for the next several years. . . . I have a blueprint presented by them and over the next few years I can see how well they do in terms of their own aspirations."

Large institutions did not provide any semblance of an orientation; colleges and departments had them in keeping with the comments above. At small institutions, there was often an all-college orientation, but again, such activities were usually regarded as bureaucratic exercises. A small liberal arts college held a "new faculty orientation seminar" that met once a week from September to March to familiarize new faculty with the college's unique curriculum and teaching approaches. This orientation was centered on teaching and learning and included sessions on "issues of gender, race, age, ethnicity across the curriculum," "active learning," "theory and methodology across the disciplines," "taking the liberal arts into the world of jobs and careers," "conversations with master teachers," "the uses of discussion, lecture, peer-teaching, workshops, independent study," etc. Junior faculty had mixed feelings about the orientation. An African American said, "I wouldn't make it so packed with information. . . . I would have liked someone to talk about the culture of the college . . . and a mentor to tell us how to steer through the university." A woman learned through the orientation session not to disagree with senior faculty: "I think it's risky to present views that contradict the ideas of the senior faculty who run the seminars and lead the discussions. . . . You have to have the political sense to figure out, 'What is this person's agenda?' 'What is this person's personal views on this?' and then say things that are consistent with that, because you don't know if that person is going to be on your tenure review committee or not." Another woman said, "All these brochures that tell me the students' SATs and GPAs don't tell me who the students really are." Another described the orientation somewhat disdainfully as being told "what kinds of assignments to give, how to lead a discussion, how to organize a syllabus, etc." She said, "We are taught how to 'engineer' the classroom." A male professor said, "It is sort of a formal attempt to socialize you into the ethos of the place, but there doesn't seem to be much intellectual discussion across disciplinary boundaries. . . . There doesn't seem to be as much introduction of one's intellectual *self* to people in other disciplines." An advanced junior faculty explained the orientation as a bonding ritual: "It's just like those people who dance to get rain . . . it creates solidarity, it doesn't give you the rain. . . . The orientation does not teach you how to teach but it functions as a space to get to know each other."

Orientation meetings and junior faculty retreats that were scheduled at the beginning of the semester and were intended to relieve the anxiety of being a newcomer at times had the opposite effect. A woman on her first month on the job said,

> I just don't know how I'm surviving this month, it was awful. I was working seven days a week . . . Saturday's and Sunday's, except for Yom Kippur. . . . I didn't leave time for my husband to get his work done. And I didn't see much of the children and they are kind of homesick . . . and money is tight . . . and the retreat and orientation are all happening at the same time that you are preparing for classes.

The larger the institution, the less likely it was that a new faculty member would meet a vice president or the president. Again, in a system with the abundance of institutions that we have in the United States, it would be a mistake to suggest that every one of them should have a rigid system in place for the orientation of new faculty. Some individuals will find phone calls during the summer from a departmental chair unnecessary, and others will not need any help in getting their work under way. At the same time, if we are to apply the critical postmodern framework described in chapter 1, we might consider how the "cultural capital" of initiates is developed, and what might be done to ensure that newcomers do not feel excluded by their organizations. At the minimum, we consider how an institution might develop a more coordinated schema of entry than the haphazard process described here.

Organizational Socialization

Mentoring

One of the more widely discussed aspects of academic life for junior faculty is who, if anyone, offered advice about one's work. With regard to what is commonly known as "mentoring," how individuals spoke about what they needed, what they found, and who provided support fell into a variety of different categories. The notion of a single experienced faculty member being willing and able to play the all-inclusive role of mentor to a protege is wishful thinking. As we shall see, a variety of individuals help to meet a new faculty member's diverse needs. We shall divide mentoring into two categories—formal and informal—to differentiate between those aspects of socialization that occur when both parties acknowledge that mentoring is taking place, and when one or both parties may be unaware of it.

Formal

"I learned that I needed more than one person," said one individual, "because one person is good for one thing and not another." He then went on to list his multiple needs: "The department chair helps with advice about how to get things done around here, and that's good, but he's no help at all on my research or where to get things published. And he's abysmal about politics with the dean. So I've found different people for each problem."

These comments are instructive in two ways. First, the individual that was mentioned most often with regard to mentoring was the departmental chair. Second, individuals often found mentors outside their department, and at times, even outside their school or college. It is fairly common for a departmental chair to be looked on as a mentor. Indeed, more than one peer echoed this business school dean: "I don't have time to get to know all of the junior faculty personally. My department chairs are really the front line. They're the ones who care and nurture the younger faculty."

Some chairs were well-meaning but lacked the organization and leadership to make mentoring an established practice. A man said, "As far as mentoring, our division chair has suggested that new faculty form a mentoring committee, but it's not really going anywhere. . . . I've asked a couple of people who've said, 'Aw, gee, I haven't got enough time for that.' So, I'm not sure what to do next."

After the departmental chair, the most typical working relationship was a senior professor assigned to act as a mentor to someone in his/her own department. On occasion a tenured faculty member from another department would assume this responsibility. The success of a departmental chair or a senior professor in this capacity was often limited. "I was assigned someone," related one person, "but it's very stilted. Really not much help." Another individual made the same point: "The kind of mentoring that we're talking about takes some bonding, and to just assign somebody usually is a disaster, or at least of minimal support." A third person simply stated, "I have never asked for advice. It shows weakness, and I won't do that."

At the same time, some relationships did work. One assistant professor spoke about a senior professor in her department in the following manner:

> There's a senior professor in my department who is really great. He has sat in my classes and met with me after class and made some points. Why did I call on the same students, for example. How I should know people's names. Be more lively. The large lecture classes can eat you alive and I've watched him do it. He's looked over my syllabi and made comments. He's written a letter for my files, but that's just going through the motions. He's concerned about making me a better teacher.

Unexpectedly, a woman at a large research university received support from a very senior man: "I connected intellectually with a professor who was viewed as cantankerous." She said, ". . . No one with whom I shared the paper gave me substantive comments and the same day I gave it to him he called me at home and gave me a lot of advice."

These individuals were the exception when junior faculty spoke about senior faculty. Most tenure-track faculty neither received formal feedback of any kind, nor did they seek assistance. One individual took a leave of absence for a year and worked in a company where she was able to get self-help videos about teaching, but she never asked for help at her institution. Another person mentioned how he kept in contact with his former classmates from graduate school and sent them drafts of his articles. A third individual was involved in an interdisciplinary reading group that provided support.

Other individuals spoke of their dissertation chairs as reliable experts. "The chair of my dissertation is a big help," said one assistant professor. "There's not really anyone here in my areas." Another person echoed this comment: "I go to someone who was on my dissertation committee who's become a friend." But someone else with a similar perspective made a startling and depressing comment. Prior to this individual's arrival on campus, she had been awarded a major fellowship that provided her with $100,000 a year for five years. During the interview, we congratulated her on having received the award. Toward the end of the session, she told us this:

> No one here has ever congratulated me like you just did. What I have heard is that my ideas are no good, or I got the award because I was a woman, or because the awards committee knew my dissertation chair.
>
> I'll tell you this, if I didn't have my dissertation chair to talk to on the telephone, I'd be lost. If I didn't have a mentor to tell me I was good, I'd be very discouraged. He provides feedback on my work, keeps in touch with me, and asks me for input on his own work, too, like a colleague. But he's at my graduate school and here I have no one. It's a very cold, very impersonal department. I do everything on my own.

Such an assessment was not uncommon. When the subject of mentoring came up with junior faculty, they usually had more to say about the lack of it than they did about what took place. "There's no mentoring that goes on here at all," declared one person. "Ask any junior faculty and we'll tell you. You learn by your mistakes, or you ask somebody a year ahead of you." "I have no idea what it takes to get promotion and tenure," said another. "It's a guessing game." "They say I need a book," commented one newcomer, "but

I don't know how to deal with publishers. I'm better at journal articles." An individual who noted that forty percent of the workload was service-related commented, "We need senior faculty who will go to the dean and get me off these committees, but they're the ones who won't do the work so I get stuck with the committees. And they also sit on P and T! There are no advocates for junior faculty." Another junior faculty member described the situation as follows:

> At another university, new hires are systematically included in grant proposals. That might be called mentorship. Here, I had to go knocking on doors just to get announcements of grant availability.

Such comments provide two insights. If a department chair can not be a helpful mentor, then junior faculty often must turn to someone else. At the same time, the kinds of advice they need often requires for multiple mentors. Someone who provides helpful suggestions on teaching may not be able to criticize one's writing. Behind all of these comments, however, lies a more troubling finding. The burden of seeking sound advice falls on the individual who needs it. The organizational structure seems to regard the department chair as the primary mentor, and when she/he cannot or will not fulfill the role, the junior faculty member is left to "twist in the wind," as one individual expressed it. A junior professor mentioned that the chair of her department told all new faculty to form a mentoring committee, "but it is not really going anywhere." She also pointed out that the chair is always helpful when she has a very specific question but "he would never come around and say: 'Well, you know, give a talk here' or 'Don't you think you should go to this meeting, or that meeting.' He just doesn't do that and it would be nice if I could get a little more input as to what is appropriate and what's not." At a different institution, a woman chair said, "I see my role as initiating young people into the community . . . but," she admitted, "I do that more readily with women than with men. . . . I'm not quite sure why, it could simply be that women have a way of relating to each other that I'm familiar with, and so I'm able to communicate with the young women more easily."

At one institution senior faculty were cautious about their mentoring roles and responsibilities, according to a division head; ". . . There are some questions that [senior] faculty have about the legal status of the mentoring group as it is described in the faculty handbook . . . what are the legal responsibilities, obligations of the mentoring committee and what would happen if the junior faculty member being mentored did not get tenure."

Obviously, positive role models do exist. One person offered this portrait of the department chair:

He came in and talked with me yesterday, as a matter of fact, and sat right where you are now. He suggests places to publish my work, reads everything I write, and gives feedback. We talk all the time. He meets with all of us. He gives me things that he thinks are helpful. He met with me after the second and fourth year review and made sure I understood what was meant. That was good, because those letters can be confusing. They write something and you can blow it out of proportion, or you might miss something. He's very easy to talk to, and he also protects the junior faculty from the fights that happen from time to time in the department.

Surely, most junior faculty would rather have this individual as departmental chair than the one who "never made eye contact the one time I met with him the whole first year," as one person said. But not every departmental chair or senior professor can be as insightful and accommodating as the individual described above, and not every junior faculty member wants or needs such a mentor. One of the challenges of mentoring is matching the recipient's needs with the provider's strengths. Obviously, this kind of mentoring would require a concerted effort on the part of the department, and such was not the experience of the vast majority of respondents in this study.

Informal

Mentoring need not take place only in a senior faculty member's office or at an orientation session at the beginning of the school year. The mail room, the faculty lounge, and any number of other institutional locations have potential for socializing individuals to the culture of the department and organization. On one hand, for example, a junior faculty member commented, "There's a place where we all gather for lunch that's just down the hall. I've really enjoyed going there because we talk about our teaching problems, and it's very relaxed and very informative. It's probably the best information I've gotten." On the other hand, another person said, "A senior faculty member told me that I 'should get out more.' I didn't know what he meant. So that only made me more paranoid than I already am. I'm an outsider, and I don't know how to break in." A man at a liberal arts college with a strong teaching mission also spoke about the informal means of learning how to be a good teacher: "We get together . . . we talk . . . we ask, 'How do you do this?' 'How do you do that?' and 'Oh, by the way, I make my students do this.'" At this institution exchanges among faculty across disciplines are facilitated by the organization of the work space: "We can talk to different people from different departments . . . we are not compartmentalized . . . we have offices in the same place so there is a lot of possibility for learning from each other without having any kind of formal instruction."

A male professor in a small college said ". . . I was the first openly gay faculty member here and that was sort of a strange position to be in. . . . I feel sort of a little bit of a token in the way the president treats me. I was invited to a meeting and when I got there it was only me, the head of the trustee board and the president. I think he wanted to reassure me or the trustee that this was a good campus for people of all persuasions. . . . He treats me like I'm an example of diversity. And that gets a little bit tiresome. . . . It's also funny because the male professors who are straight sort of feel like I have some advantage or preferential treatment."

For some women interaction with senior faculty was non-existent: "I have never once been asked out for lunch. Not once. I see all the guys moving through the hall, and no one ever asks." For others it depended on their willingness to learn new behaviors: "Women tend to make dates. Men don't do that. You just barge in and say, 'Let's go to lunch.' I've had to learn that." The point, of course, is not that one individual is right and the other is wrong, but rather, might it be possible to make socialization more of a shared responsibility. Now it seems an encoded system of behavior in which newcomers must learn to survive by trial and error. There were also faculty who resisted the pressure to be visible. At a small liberal arts college a woman said, "I like to have a separation between what I do professionally and my personal life . . . sometimes I feel pressure that I shouldn't be that way. . . . I know it might be detrimental but I don't care, I'm not that kind of person."

Informal mentoring can be as simple as helping an individual network at a conference, or as complex as explaining how to navigate the cultural terrain of school and college politics. At one institution, for example, there is a longstanding tradition that at a particular time during the day faculty congregate in the cafeteria for a coffee break. As a senior professor noted, "It's not something you have to do, but it's a good way for a new person to get known, to be seen. It's a mistake to avoid it, and when there's a new person in my department, I take him there myself the first couple of times." A new professor in another department commented, "With all I've got to do, I don't see the worth of it, and I don't go. It's a waste of my time, a throwback to another era." Perhaps if the latter individual understood the symbolic significance of this tradition he might have a different interpretation. At least a new faculty member should have the opportunity to learn about this practice and decide for him or herself, which again suggests the importance of informal mentoring.

What might one make of these analyses of mentoring? In chapter 2, we mentioned various dimensions of organizational socialization that are germane to formal and informal mentoring. Orientation is a *formal* and *collec-*

tive socializing experience, whereas having coffee with a senior faculty member to discuss an idea for a joint research project is *informal* and *individual*. All these experiences involve the newcomer with senior faculty in some fashion. One way to structure the multiple roles of mentoring is to think of the mentor from three perspectives, that of (a) the symbolic leader, (b) the trail guide, and (c) the oral historian (Tierney and Rhoads 1993, 53).

Senior faculty, whether they be chairs, academic administrators, or professors in a department, have the ability to set standards by adhering to those standards themselves. Mentoring involves more than dispensing advice and imparting wisdom. If individuals learn by example, then one way junior faculty will come to understand the organizational culture is by observing the actions of those in leadership positions. The importance of teaching, collaborative work, and positive interaction with colleagues is as much learned from the act itself as from telling someone what to expect. As one newcomer remarked, "They say teaching's important here, but the senior faculty work from old course notes, and I know they don't prepare. That's a strange way to pick up things, but it helped me understand how I should be spending my time."

At the same time, individuals who enter a new culture will always have questions, and senior faculty will often find themselves cast in the role of mentor or trusted colleague. How should I handle a difficult student? Is it permissible to disagree in faculty meetings? What's more important—an article or a presentation? How do I juggle all the tasks that I've been given? These are questions that any junior faculty might have, and someone in the organization should be able and willing to provide the answers.

To those of us who have been assimilated into the academic culture, such questions may seem trivial and mundane. However, they require more than a simple yes or no answer. These are precisely the issues that define the organizational culture. The junior professor who skips meetings because he thinks they are a waste of time, or the assistant professor who wears shorts and sandals when everyone else wears business attire, creates unnecessary problems. When a tourist visits a foreign country, most often, cultural transgressions are not purposeful. Like the foreigner, the new professor usually learns a cultural rule only after he or she has broken it. The experienced colleague who takes the role of a trail guide, then, is a source of professional and cultural information.

Finally, all institutions have histories. History should not be used to fossilize an institution, but rather to help explain how it came to be what it is today. An institution bereft of history is without clear markers of identity and ideology. The analysis of the past prepares junior and senior colleagues to take on the challenges of the future. In each of these roles, a senior professor is able to impart more than wisdom or mere information; he or she can also explain how faculty members can work with one another. If history is used merely as a pretext for maintaining the status quo, then new faculty learn one thing about the institution; if it is used as a way to illustrate how contexts have changed over time so that faculty are able to change accordingly, then we learn another. The point, then, is not simply that mentoring is needed, but that we need to consider how the role is assumed so that new faculty are not mentored hierarchically, but instead are allowed to develop their own voices and academic identities.

Faculty Work

As noted in chapter 1, a common perception of faculty over the past decade is that the professoriat is populated by selfish individuals who do whatever they please and only occasionally teach students. The assumption is that faculty work short hours and occupy their time with globe-trotting to conferences and lingering over leisurely lunches at the faculty club. Charles Sykes nicely summarizes this view of professors in his book *Profscam*, contending that "they are overpaid, grotesquely underworked, and the architects of academia's vast empires of waste" (1988, 5). Sykes based his book on celebrated cases in newspapers throughout the country. As is the case with any profession, one cannot deny that some faculty members are overpaid and some do not work hard enough.

However, based on the interviews for this book, we categorically reject the characterization of faculty as lazy snobs. The point here is not merely an academic quibble. If Sykes' portrait of faculty is correct, then what academe needs to do is to hire individuals who are more dedicated and less mercenary; the problem is clear and the solution relatively simple. Do faculty members work only seven hours per week? If so, then they are shirking their professional responsibility, and they deserve to be replaced.

Our analysis is different. As we will show, faculty work long hours and make little money for what they do. Although it is true that the manner or foci of their work may not be what a state legislature or the general citizenry want from them, the issue is fundamentally different from their being lazy. Faculty work for academic rewards that are located in a cultural and structural system. The overarching problem is not with individuals who are sluggards, but with a structure that has a skewed reward system. The solution is not to replace individuals but to change the academic culture.

Work during the academic year was characterized similarly by all faculty, regardless of institutional type or discipline: "I work seven days a week," said one individual, "and I mean seven days a week." A second person said, "I take Friday afternoons off—they're for myself, and I get Sunday mornings for my family. Other than that I work every day." "I get up by five so I can write," commented a third person, "and then I get to work by eight and stay here until about seven." Another person added, "I always leave the office by six so I can have dinner with my family, but once the kids get to sleep, I probably work another two hours. I have to. I have no choice."

Over three quarters of the faculty interviewed said they worked at least three nights a week; over ninety percent said they worked for more than four hours at least one day during the weekend.

For women faculty, working long hours may also be a way of demonstrating that they are equally committed to their careers as their male colleagues and they work hard in order to prove their single-mindedness. A woman made the following observation: "In the first year I noticed how much women faculty talked about how much they worked. It seemed to have a competitive flavor: 'I was up until two in the morning,' 'Well, I was up until three and I'm on 80 committees, and blah, blah, blah.' I got the sense that the more overworked you were the better faculty person you were."

In the summer, faculty were involved in different activities, but they were equally busy. "I have taken a week with my wife and child in August," said one fourth-year professor, "but this year and next I can't because of tenure." "I like summer because there are no meetings. I still work every day, but I don't have to work in the evenings as much; that's nice," said another individual. A third person added, "I stay home all summer, but it makes me more neurotic, frankly, because then I feel I have to work all the time. I can't remember a day last summer when I totally just vegged out." A fourth person concurred, but from a different angle; "My office is air-conditioned and the students aren't around, so I come in early, put on a pot of coffee, and get to it. The kids are home in the summer, so it's not as convenient to work at home. I actually come here more often in the summer." "Summers are a time when I feel terribly isolated and alone . . . I need to devise a system of checking in with a few people . . . I don't labor alone very well," said a man who worked more effectively when he had colleagues with whom to talk or collaborate on writing projects.

The respondents' comments made us wonder about the efficiency and nature of faculty work. Perhaps faculty are simply inefficient and need to make better use of their time. It may be that every professional works as hard as the faculty portrayed themselves working. Although in the final chapter we shall address ways that junior faculty might structure their time to increase productivity, it is also important to outline how they see their time. As one individual commented, "I'm not a factory worker. This isn't a nine-to-five job. I guess most people would say they like the freedom of faculty life, but it's a weird freedom, isn't it? The freedom to work all the time." A second person made a similar point: "Everything I do is time-consuming. If you grade papers the way you're supposed to, it takes time. They need to see your comments. And my research, my writing, is not something I just sit down and type out and I'm done. I have to think. Think. Think." Another person added, "When I'm in my lab, I can't force results. Sure, there are ways I've learned to be more efficient, but experiments and ideas are not just putting things together. It's messy." A final comment comes from a faculty member who thinks of himself as primarily a researcher:

> It's funny. I'm paid to do my research. I spend lots of time at it. But I enjoy working with students, and I make myself as available as possible to them. I even hold some office hours on Saturday mornings because I know there won't be interruptions. I have my grad students over to my house all the time. I have no time for myself, and sometimes that causes trouble at home. I've got to find a balance.

A comparative perspective on the pace of work in other professions was provided by those faculty members in business, engineering or the sciences who had been in industry or business previously. Interestingly, virtually everyone said they worked harder and spent longer hours in their academic positions. "There's no comparison," said one person. "I worked a lot in my last job, sure, but it was not like this." Another person went a step further: "My work is never-ending here, and the pace is relentless. I don't know if I can keep at it, and I am seriously considering returning to industry. Better hours, better pay." A third person stated, "I had no idea what I was in for. The problem is that you never know how much is enough, and if you want to do a good job, if you take yourself seriously, that means you just keep working. At [his business company] I knew when I had done a good job. I'd blow off steam and then start on another project. Not here." A fourth person related the pace of life to a triathlon:

> I don't know if I am a distance runner, biker and swimmer. I feel like I'm asked to do everything at once and all the time. At work I had one job, one task, and maybe one on the drawing boards. Here, you have one project going, one in planning, one or two you're writing grants for, and the constant submission/revision of articles. Then there are the students. My graduate students line up outside the door, the undergraduates want their exams back, and somebody's always in crisis. And then there's the service side where you're asked to

sit on committees. Who can do all this? Whoever thinks faculty life is the leisurely pursuit of knowledge should follow me around for a while.

These comments raise several issues to which we shall return in the concluding chapter. Faculty can undoubtedly schedule their time more productively, and some activities might be rearranged in the interest of efficiency. However, to understand how individuals might be more productive, we need to examine more closely the essential activities that account for faculty work—teaching, research and service. How do faculty construct their lives in each domain, and what is their perception of each activity?

Teaching

"I'm not good at giving tests," admitted one assistant professor, "and yes, I know there's an instructional development center on campus. After tenure, I'll probably go there. I don't have time now." "I heard of one person who was told her teaching scores were too high," said another untenured faculty member. "If your scores are too high, it means you're spending too much time on teaching." "I like to teach," commented a third person, "but it's not valued." A fourth person said, "I'm a perfectionist, and the system doesn't like it. I'm an okay teacher. I get good scores, but I could be better, but if I spent my time improving, I wouldn't get tenure." A fifth person added, "You're going for competence in teaching. In research, you have to go for superiority." A sixth person said, "When I got here, I knew nothing about teaching. I knew my area, how to write grants, even how to publish. But teaching was, and remains, something of a mystery."

In small institutions where teaching is the most salient activity, a professor's accessibility to students is one of the many tacit forms of judging whether a new professor embodies desirable qualities. A male professor at a liberal arts college said, "As an undergraduate I would have never walked up to a professor's office and just knocked on the door and expected that professor to drop everything and sit and talk to me . . . but that is the almost uniform expectation here." However, as this professor found out, in a student-centered institution students will use teaching evaluations as a means of sanctioning an indifferent professor. "I started off being resistant . . . I set specific hours, I would not leave my door open. . . . If students came by and I was busy I would tell them I was busy . . . but when students wrote in their evaluations 'the professor is not available, or never available, or won't talk to me,' I began to change my attitude and have tried to adapt to the culture of the college." A woman professor agreed, "They want to see the professor on campus five days a week . . . they want you visible."

The smaller, private institutions valued teaching more than the research universities did; but theirs was a curious valuation largely as a result of the manner in which teaching is assessed. "To be honest," said one provost, "we're not very systematic. You'd think in a small place we would be clear about what is expected. We're not." His faculty echoed his concern. "Someone comes into my class once a semester and writes something up that goes into my file, and that's about it." A senior professor explained how the faculty recognize good teaching: "We always use the scores students give faculty, but in a place our size, you just know. Osmosis. Students won't take their classes, or there's talk. We all sort of know who's good and who's not." Another senior professor at another institution with a similar process disagreed: "It's a mystery to me that faculty can write evaluations about someone when they have never been to the person's class, they may never have read an article of the individual's. All they have to go on is hall talk and student evaluations, word of mouth. The system is due for an overhaul."

Student evaluations were given much credence in every institution we visited. "My advice to a new person," reflected one person, "is don't be a crummy teacher. Being good is nice, but not important. That means get a score above the mean." A department chair in another institution said she was quite explicit in what she told her faculty: "Our rating scale on the student evaluation is 1–4. We have one question that asks, 'How would you rate this professor with other faculty you have had?' I tell everyone that they need to get a 2.9 or above." An individual ironically confirmed that was what he had been told: "It's screwy. Here we are a science school and we're working as if this is Lake Woebegone—all the faculty are above average." However, the desire to be above average was fairly common. At another institution, "Question 14" set the standard. "We all know it as soon as we come in," said one junior professor wryly. " 'How'd you do on 14?' you'll say to someone at the end of the semester who's a friend. Only a friend, though, because it's such a personal question. 'Are you above average?' " In a research university one of the colleges published the names of the faculty who were ranked in the top twenty percent; an assistant professor who was number three on the list said, "People seem to take teaching evaluations seriously. . . . One of the professors who is very productive and doesn't seem to care much about teaching seems to care about getting good evaluations. . . . He used to discourage students from coming to see him during office hours but now he has made some changes so that students will like him better and therefore give him more positive evaluations."

A man at a major research university who admitted to "especially liking undergraduate teaching" said, "It was clear in my mind from things that were said in the interview that research came first far and away, and as long as I held up the my end of the research, if I wanted to be a good teacher, too, that was ok." He added, the "research culture" came through in comments such as, "you don't want to teach undergraduates," "students are a nuisance," and "constant talk about research, research goals, and research needs and very little about teaching."

A woman whose teaching evaluations were "terrible" and was criticized by students for not making the "material more structured and quantifiable" said, ". . . They [other faculty and academic administrators] expect you to do so much, to take the pulse of the group dynamics of the classroom, and kind of minister to the students who lack self-esteem . . . and I'm finding it rather exhausting to imagine teaching in a place where so much of your energy has to be devoted to that."

"I hate to say this," said one person, "but you learn tricks to up your average. Give a midterm assessment is one. Sure, it will help you improve. It will also up your average at the end of the semester because students feel they're included. It's cynical." A faculty member at a research institution offered a word of caution about being above average: "If you excel at teaching, someone will undoubtedly think you're putting too much into your teaching and you should be doing research. So my advice is to be good, but not great." On the other hand, a man in another research university on his first year as assistant professor said, "This year I have spent most of my time on teaching. I take teaching very seriously and it shows up in my evaluations. . . . I am looking at the time I put into teaching as 'start up costs'"

The greatest concern of junior faculty was having to teach large lecture sections. "I got eaten alive my first semester," said one person. Another individual said, "I had my class in the afternoon, and I watched a senior professor teach in the morning. It was like a dress rehearsal." A third person said, "I'm good with discussions, but lectures really scared me. The department chair provided me [with] previous lecture notes, and that helped some, but I still get nervous." A fourth person summarized, "You don't know how to teach, and in graduate school you really don't think about it. A discussion class is difficult, but it's manageable. A large class is like a production, and since teaching is not very important here anyway, it's a lose-lose situation. You feel you should spend time, but you don't, so you go into class having spent too much time, but not enough time, and they grow restless."

At one institution a young professor with very little teaching experience suggested having a "voluntary observation system" among junior faculty but none of his colleagues were interested in pursuing the idea.

Our point here is that faculty are socialized about teaching in the most haphazard way. They may never have taught a class before they arrive at their respective institutions, and depending on the predilection of their department chair, they may or may not receive advice about how to construct a course. Tenure is a system of evaluation, so they are evaluated for their teaching; but the assessment is based on individual and particularistic notions that reveal more about the idiosyncrasies of the evaluator than about a communal agreement as to what constitutes good teaching. The fundamental lesson, however, is that teaching is not that important; if it were, there would be more discussions about what constitutes good teaching.

Research

The excuse for lack of involvement in teaching centers on research. "What does it take to get tenure?" asked one person. "That's the million dollar question. Standards change, and you never know how many articles you need." Another person said, "Everybody talks about it. It feeds on itself. Someone gets published, and you feel sort of good for the person but frantic about yourself." "I have over 20 articles in refereed journals," said another person, "but people keep telling me I need a book. The dean wants a book." At a research university senior faculty who want to discourage the "counting mentality" were proposing to change the evaluation system so that each faculty would submit "three or four articles that reflect the best in their corpus of their work . . . the kinds of publications that will have a continuing impact on their field."

Asked, "What do you have to do to get tenure here?" a man said: "I don't know. I haven't really worried about any concrete quantitative measure of output even if one exists. I figure, 'I will work as hard as I can.' I will work as hard as I can, and then whatever happens, happens."

"I had a book contract," commented someone else, "and in my second year review, they said I should concentrate on articles, not the book. So I did. In my fourth year review, they said, 'Where's the book?'" "I publish," said one person, "but I've been told I publish in the wrong journals. That's because I'm in a field that is in between." Another person added, "I'm in business, but my field is in psychology, so about half my work is published in psychological journals. My department chair told me that was fine." His dean said, "What advice would I give to a young faculty member? I'd tell them to publish in business journals. We are a professional field and we should service the profession. To publish elsewhere would be a risk." A faculty member in finance at another institution echoed this concern: "I have published articles in accounting, and now I'm worried because I've been told they may not count for tenure in my field." The chair of a department that had just denied tenure to an assistant professor with 17 published articles said, "They were really lousy articles in professional level journals . . . the kind of journal that publishes your picture along with the article and it is on shiny paper . . . articles written for a lay audience do not meet with great acceptance."

Perhaps the faculty who face the most difficult time with research are those in the sciences and engineering. "It's a Catch-22," said one. "I have to publish, and in order to publish, I have to have graduate students who need a lab, which takes a major grant." "I spend fifty percent of my time writing grants," said another person. "They give you $50,000 to get started here, and it's not enough. Science costs money; the federal government doesn't have the money anymore," said another. "Senior faculty think that we can do what they did when they were young, and they continue to do now that they are old, but it's different now. They're well-known so they get money, and for new faculty there's just nothing out there." "Tenure's going to change," concluded another, "but it will not change in the near future." Another individual commented, "I've been told point blank that I have to bring in money or I won't get tenure." A provost at another institution was equally straightforward: "If someone in the sciences doesn't get a significant grant or two, it's inconceivable that they'll get tenure." A woman said, "I require a fair amount of technical support in the form of instrumentation, to pursue the scholarship that I'm trained for, and it is an issue because in science research activities tend to be more expensive."

In general, faculty at every type of institution enjoyed research, although they tended to steer clear of ground-breaking work because it took too long. They needed to write articles, and in the interest of accumulating publications, an individual could not devote years to a project that might not yield results. "I want to get tenure," said one, "and that makes me risk averse. I could go down one road that might lead to a big breakthrough in my field, but it also might lead nowhere. So I go for little results that get me publications." Another individual commented, "I do gay and lesbian work, and that will probably be my downfall. It's not seen as relevant. But that's what I want to do, so that's life." A third person commented, "They want me to get published in journals that have low acceptance rates, so that says to me, play it safe." A political scientist said, "There are three journals that are taken seriously. . . . I just published an article in the premier journal and that probably has done more for my standing in this department than anything else."

Sometimes faculty get conflicting messages; their colleagues might say one thing and the chair might say something completely different. Additionally, there are inconsistencies between what an institution claims to value and what it regards as worthy of being rewarded. For example, in a liberal arts teaching-oriented institution a woman who wrote an article on the institution's distinctive pedagogical practices in the sciences said in a frustrated voice, "The faculty committee did not think the article was very valuable. It was anecdotal, I wrote about how I teach, how I deal with students and they said, 'Well, it doesn't have any analytical depth.'" She said, "It is confusing to me as to what counts . . . I came here to teach science and I want to write about innovative methods that I am trying to implement. . . . I am not really interested in investigating theories of education." Ironically, this institution had embraced Boyer's (1990) notion of the "scholarship of teaching" but when the professor asked for greater clarification an academic administrator told her:

> Well, you know when you talk about the scholarship of teaching, if you would like to do a study you need to have a control group and you have another group who gets the treatment and you analyze what happens. . . . That would fit into the scholarship of teaching.

Apparently at this institution the "scholarship of teaching" was interpreted to signify the "science of teaching."

At a research university a junior faculty was unsure whose advice to follow, the senior members of the faculty who said, ". . . Forget about service, forget about teaching—go for your research," or senior academic administrators who countered, "Well, no: You ought to be teaching a lot of undergraduate courses."

Nevertheless, most individuals felt that research held some interest for them. As one person at a research university noted, "About fifty percent of my time is spent doing research, and I think that's about right. I just wish I could spend that fifty percent slightly differently." The person's comment reflected a desire to concentrate less on publishing and more on research. As one person summarized:

> Things take so long. You send something to an "A" journal—that's the big thing now—and you wait to hear. And then you get it accepted after making revisions, but no one says anything. It's like, what are you working on now? You know the saying 'publish or perish'? I know what they mean. But the pace is too much. It's the non-stop race. It's not conducive to good work because you have to rush to get things out. In my darker moments, I think I will probably 'publish *and* perish.'

A woman at a small liberal arts college said that when she interviewed for the position her "understanding was that research was very important." But when she began to work at the college she found that "yes, publishing is important but you have to find your own time to do the research and it should not get in the way of any other activities having to do with students, whether extracurricular or curricular." Additionally, at this institution faculty were encouraged and rewarded for collaborative research projects that involved undergraduate students. A woman said, "I supervised three, four or five separate projects and all the students went to a conference to present the results. The university paid the airfare and lodging for a student whose project was accepted for presentation at a national conference." Even though this institution rewards faculty-student research collaboration, this professor complained: "It takes so much energy away from my own research interests that I have gravitated more towards picking my own line of research and getting students involved by hiring them as research assistants." She also voiced concern about how this kind of research would affect her marketability: "Now, I prefer to make clear that the students are my assistants rather than me being an assistant on the students' projects. I've become more focused on making myself marketable outside this institution and the collaborative research projects do not enhance my curriculum vitae."

Service

Service was the least valued activity in all institutions, but the expectations for service varied more than any other domain. That is to say, at every institution we visited everyone was expected to teach and conduct some research. Obviously, the faculty member in the small liberal arts institution may only have had to publish one article over the course of a one- or two-year period, whereas such an output would have been insufficient at the large research university. However, with service, some faculty were not expected to do anything, and others were called on repeatedly. In the next two chapters, we will elaborate in greater detail the overuse of women and faculty of color in this domain, but at this point, let us consider what service meant both symbolically and with regard to time and effort.

One rule of thumb might be that smaller institutions expect more service than larger institutions do; and in larger institutions service generally remains within the department whereas in smaller colleges new faculty will serve on committees that address institution-wide issues as well as the concerns of their own department. At a small institution, for example, we heard: "I am on about six committees, and two of them are in my department. Two are for the school, and two more are all-college." Another person said, "You just get put on them from the vice president's office. It's like you have to take your turn." A third person countered, "I like campus committees because it's a way to meet people."

At a small liberal arts college junior faculty in the first three years of their appointment are assigned the social activities that at one time had been sponsored by the "Faculty Wives' Committee." A male professor said, "We are responsible for the punch and cookies for faculty meetings . . . we have to organize an international dinner in the fall for all the faculty and collect dues to support the social life of the faculty." For many faculty, planned social activities are one more thing they have to comply with and show they can be part of the college community. A woman who went along with this social duty said, "I want to do well, and I want to be accepted so it is important that I be social, but it's just not my real way of being." She continued, "I want to eat where I am comfortable and with people I know . . . not with strangers. But that's my tribal way."

In a large research university, however, individuals rarely served on committees that went beyond their college. "The university is sort of a myth for me," admitted one person; "I know it's out there, but I don't have anything to do with it." Another person said, "It's really light here. I mean really light. I'm on one committee in my department, and it meets a couple of times a semester." A third person added, "The problem with committee work is that it's busy work. It takes time, so I avoid it, and in general, the department chair tries to shield me from it, too." Not everyone was this fortunate: "Almost fifty percent of my time is on committees. The problem is that we don't have enough senior faculty to go around, and those who are senior don't want to serve. The department chair feels he doesn't have a choice, and the dean seems oblivious. There are always good reasons to put me on a committee; it's just that I don't think it will help me get tenure."

Everyone agreed that service did not count in any practical sense when a candidate was being considered for tenure. One needed to show that he/she was at least minimally involved in the affairs of the department, but not much more. However, service also provided a way for senior faculty to form opinions about junior faculty, and in this sense, it became more important symbolically than practically. "My department chair told me I should get on college-wide committees," said one individual, "because that's the way faculty in the other departments get to know you." "It's not a good idea," said one department chair, "for a younger person to stay hidden away. I see it as my responsibility to put them on committees where they learn about the institution, and the rest of us learn about them." One chair of a promotion and tenure committee said, "Service is hard to evaluate when we go over someone's files, but it's also the only time, probably, that somebody in another department has had to meet the person or know what he's done. 'Oh, he served on that task force last year. That was a bear,' someone will say, and they'll think well of the candidate for it." Thus, service becomes the third aspect of faculty work that is comparably vague in its demands and assessment.

What are we to make of these portraits of faculty at work? Our summary consists of three main points. First, junior faculty spend long hours trying to meet multiple responsibilities. Second, the tasks that are set for them—teaching, research and service—are often ill-defined and poorly evaluated. Third, an individual's activity is often devoid of any overriding sense of institutional purpose or identity, for if the purpose were to achieve excellence in teaching, then such activities would be rewarded. These findings are both commonplace and controversial.

The contention that faculty work hard contradicts the armchair diatribes of authors such as Sykes or Kimball. To suggest that a teacher's task is ill-defined when it is clear that he or she is assigned to teach X number of courses over a 15-week semester seems odd as well. At the same time, calls for greater accountability and assessment of faculty teaching have become commonplace during the past. To express concern that individual activity is not related to institutional ideology is to suggest that an institution should have a unifying purpose. Authors such as Clark (1987) or Becher (1987) would disagree, for their work accentuates the importance of one's discipline and they depict the institution as little more than a holding company in which the professoriat pursue their intellectual interests.

Our point is that one first needs data in order to analyze a situation. The interviewed individuals offered convincing evidence that they work hard. Tasks are ill-defined because they lack what we called in chapter 1 an overarching "intellectual perspective." Institutions are unsure of their mission, and in turn faculty are not sure what to do, or how to evaluate their own work and the work of their colleagues. To say that colleges and universities are uncertain about assessing faculty work is not necessarily a call for more evaluation. Rather, as we noted in chapter 1, the institution needs to develop a "strategic perspective" that evolves from an institutional mission and purpose. However, in our actual investigation of the actual process of tenure evaluation, we have found individuals who are confounded by a process that obscures the institutional purpose rather than helping to define it.

The Tenure Process

In chapter 2, we outlined several different tenure scenarios. Although the process appears straightforward—a candidate compiles a dossier, and a cadre of individuals and groups vote on it—the vast majority of assistant professors are either confused by the process or unaware of what is needed. As one noted, "I don't know why everything needs to be so secretive." The lack of clarity and confusion was as much of a problem for individuals we interviewed at small institutions as for those at large ones, and as much for faculty in the humanities and social sciences as for faculty in engineering, business, or the sciences. Our principal concern here is that most candidates have neither a clear understanding of how the process works nor of the time frame. For example, a woman who had just gone through her third-year review at a small liberal arts college told us,

> That year the review was just a mess so it wasn't particularly helpful. . . . They wanted names of three potential reviewers and so I did my research about people who were in appropriate institutions and so on and submitted the names. Then some time passed and finally I got word that all the reviewers had to be local and none of the reviewers I had given them were local. That meant that in a matter of two or three days I had to come up with new names. It was incredibly stressful.

We noted in the previous section, for example, that one individual who had only written articles felt he needed to have published a book to support his case for tenure. Another candidate thought it was satisfactory to write for journals outside his field, yet his dean said the opposite. One person who was up for fourth-year review said, "I have a book chapter, a conference paper and I'm about to submit an article to a journal." Someone else in the same college said, "They want refereed articles and nothing else." At another college, a person commented, "I'm trying to get a few articles from my dissertation," but another person cautioned, "Stay away from your dissertation. It won't count. That's what I've been told." A librarian said, "They think all we do is check out books, which is unfair, but so is our workload. We're held to faculty standards for publications and administrative standards for work." An assistant professor at a research university who had just gone through his fourth-year review said, "I don't know how much I need to do but I know that if I went for tenure now, I would not have a prayer. I need to get a lot of stuff published between now and then. . . . They just don't look at quantity; they pay a lot of attention to where you are publishing."

One individual who had spent a significant amount of time in service said, "I haven't published very much, but my service is the best in the college and my teaching is good. I think they'll take that into account." However, one of her colleagues contended, "Service counts for nothing." A business professor who had attained tenure during the course of the two year study said, "I've won two teaching awards, but I also have 15 articles." A younger professor commented, "I heard he got tenure because of his teaching, so I'm going to concentrate more on teaching." In another institution, an assistant professor said, "I don't think that any of my junior faculty cronies are under any illusions about the importance of research versus teaching."

Equally troubling was the variability of candidate opinions on good outside reviewers. When asked, If the dean suggested that they apply for tenure immediately, whom would they ask for letters of support? One assistant professor described his game plan as follows:

> I'm cultivating names. I have been working on that since day one. When I complete an article I send it to a list I have of ten to fifteen people. I always send my work to them. People need to know you. If you haven't thought about the process, you don't see this. I also go to four conferences a year. I network. There's always more than one reason you do something; it takes time for people to know you, to know your work, and they have to know you. There's nothing worse than getting an outside letter that begins, "I've never heard of this person."

Few other junior faculty members seemed as well prepared or self-confident as this person. Some had thought about the process but had not developed a strategy: "I want to use someone who was on my dissertation committee, but he's at another university. Is that okay?" Another person said, "Someone asked me to write a chapter in a book, and I'd like to use her, but I guess I can't. I don't know who I'll use." A fourth-year assistant professor said, "I've just started thinking about it. I know two people." A candidate who had gone through the process said, "They need twelve names here, and who knows? How can you get a dozen people to know your work? You should start working on it as soon as you start, but most of us don't think about it until it's too late."

We found similar confusion with regard to the evaluation and documentation of teaching. "I've kept all my syllabi," explained one individual. "In three years, a handful of students have written notes saying they liked my class, and I've kept them in a file folder. A faculty member from another department lectured in my class and told me afterward he thought the class was well prepared. I asked him to write a note about it. I know it sounds hokey, but I was told to do it." Another person commented, "I suppose the evaluations of the departmental faculty are what they judge me on, and the student scores." A third person summarized, "The scores. Nothing else." A fourth person in the same department said, "You need to write a brief philosophy statement about your teaching. Why you do what you do. I've really thought about it." A fifth person said, "I haven't thought about what goes into any of this. This is only my second year and I'll get to it in a few years."

The six-year time frame for tenure in general, and the one-year tenure process in particular, were also confusing to individuals. A junior faculty member at a large university with multiple levels of tenure review, believed that if the college committee and the dean voted for tenure, then it was conferred automatically. Another person thought the process "concluded sometime in early January," when actually it did not end until May. Another person thought she had to have her materials ready by the first day of classes in the fall, when in fact she did not need them until October. At another institution, three candidates who thought they needed to compile their papers by October were told in July to get them ready by August.

Variations in the tenure process were also a mystery. One individual who had never heard of early tenure was offered a tenured position elsewhere, and planned to leave the institution although she would have preferred to stay. Another person thought he had credit toward tenure for years at his previous institution, only to discover that he was mistaken when he was turned down because the institution only granted "early tenure" to exceptional candidates. One individual decided to "stop out" for a year because of health reasons, and someone else in a similar situation in the same institution did not know that such a policy existed.

The end result is that people stagger to the end of the tenure review. Rather than feeling elated if they attain tenure, they feel relieved. "I have a serious case of tenuritis," glumly said a person who was the first to be granted tenure in his school in ten years. "It's been dehumanizing. There's tremendous soul searching that goes on, but it's not productive because you always end up thinking you're not good enough. I'm disheartened by the whole thing." An individual in another institution summarized: "I've got it. I will never give it up, because I would never put myself or my family through that again. Never." The individual who was turned down for early tenure said, "I never knew single-authored articles in refereed journals were what I should do. Fine. I will resign from every committee I'm on and put minimal effort into my teaching. I've learned my lesson." A person who did not get tenure said, "No one ever sat me down. I hate saying that, because it's my responsibility. I failed. It's my failure." An individual who had a successful publishing record but had not brought in grants said, "I feel ashamed. I should have gotten a grant and I did not."

Similarly, it is disturbing to hear the perceptions of faculty about how they should act: "My advice would be to keep your head down and mouth shut." "Don't trust anybody," said another person, and a third commented, "Watch people closely. Observe what goes on so you're sure you do just what they [senior faculty] do."

Are these the kind of comments we want to hear from individuals who have gone through the tenure process? Individual responsibility is necessary in any organization or community, but in a community such as the one we described in the first chapter responsibility is shared. Participants in institutions ought not to be allowed to absolve themselves of responsibility when an a junior faculty member fails to achieve tenure. "Soul searching" should be done not only by an individual trying to attain tenure, but also with regard to how the participants structure the work place. If we create a system where tenure is placed in high regard, then individuals at least ought to have the right to feel a sense that they accomplished a difficult task. Instead, individuals feel relieved, as if an illness is in remission. Further, what are the consequences for the organization when individuals either achieve or do not achieve tenure, but have been socialized to norms such as described in this chapter?

As with any qualitative research, some readers may question the validity of particularistic comments. Should policies be created based on one individual's perception? The response is different from simply answering yes or no. We have tried to draw accurate portraits based on the data. Even so, individuals sometimes made contradictory statements: "The department chair met me at the airport. I thought that was great," said one person; but another person said, "They should have an assistant professor meet somebody when he arrives so it's not so threatening." The easiest response to such data is to contend no one response is correct. However, our point throughout this text is that at a minimum the participants in an organization need to develop strategic responses to replace the haphazard activities that seem to be the norm at present.

In chapter 6, we shall discuss what we mean by strategic responses in greater detail and offer suggestions for developing a different process of socialization. For now, however, we shall turn to an even more uncomfortable task. We shall delineate the particular problems faced by women faculty and faculty of color as they undergo the processes that have been outlined.

CHAPTER 4

(EN)Gender(ING) Socialization

"I had two offers. At the first place, when I went for the interview I met the chair, and the man who will be the next chair, and the man who is the dean, and the man who's been in the department the longest time, and the man who teaches religion, and it was like a little club of men. I just met with the senior men in the department. I didn't meet any junior faculty. I didn't meet any women. I know there were women in the department, but they didn't schedule me to meet any of them. They didn't take me out to dinner the night before. They didn't give me breakfast. I assumed that there was an internal candidate and they were just going through the motions. But they ended up offering me the job.

"Two days later, I came for the interview here, and it was like sunshine after rain. It was the most thoughtful of all of the five campus interviews. They did things like giving me twenty minutes to myself between meetings with people. At the other place, I had forty-five minute meetings with people starting at eight thirty in the morning and going through until seven at night without a break. Here people escorted me from one place to another, so that I got to meet people without feeling as if they were interviewing me. In my schedule they had the names of the persons that would take me to each meeting and the name of the person who would pick me up. At the other place, I actually wrote the schedule down myself while the chair read it to me."

This woman was more fortunate than the man we introduced in the previous chapter. Having received only one offer, he was obliged to accept a position in an institution that made him uneasy. She received job offers from both institutions, giving her a choice. As might have been expected, she accepted the position in the latter institution and told the chair at the former one that she was declining their offer because "I can't imagine what it would be like to walk into that department every day."

In view of the inconsiderate treatment this applicant received at the former institution, her decision did not come as a surprise. What surprised us, however, was that she rejected it even though she was offered $7,000 more than the salary she is receiving at her present institution.

It is commonly assumed that faculty search committees know how to conduct a campus visit so that the candidate leaves with the impression that their institution would be a good place to begin or continue one's academic career. When the interview involves a woman or a minority group member and the search committee is all male and/or all white, what is said and done is viewed through the lenses of gender and race. A department conveys significant messages about its culture and the climate for women when a sexist remark made by a member of the search committee is greeted with chuckles, or the candidate is told by a senior professor that he will have to skip the interview luncheon because he has a tennis date, or very few of the senior faculty show up for the candidate's job talk, or the all-male faculty spends more time arguing with one another than talking with the candidate.

Our interviews with administrative leaders and department chairs suggest that senior faculty, the great majority of whom are white males, are unaware of the gendered and racial connotations of their conduct, language, mode of interaction, gestures, etc. Often senior faculty and administrators mistakenly assume that being blind to gender or race assures women and minority applicants that they will be given equal consideration and judged solely on the basis of merit and credentials. Indeed, the interview excerpts with which we opened the previous chapter and this one support this view: Men and women can be subjected to equally bad interview situations. However, the cumulative effect of patronizing, sexist, or tactless behavior on the part of an all-male search committee has unique implications for women in that it compels them to function in a climate that is neither supportive nor affirming.

In the previous chapter, we discussed the tenure and promotion years; in this one we shall focus on the particular experiences of women[1]. We contend that gender equity and nonsexist academic workplaces cannot be attained unless conscious attention is given to relations between men and women. We wish to dispel the widely held belief that gender blindness—the claim that the professor's sex is invisible—constitutes equal treatment for female and male academics. To the contrary, we maintain that the eradication of overt and covert discrimination against women requires critical and gender-based appraisals of academic structures, practices, and policies as well as the elimination of language and interactions that create overtly hostile, patronizing, or indifferent workplaces for women. Our premise is that the relations between men and women at the departmental and institutional levels create different socialization experiences. In this chapter we use gender as the lens to analyze the impact on women of socialization practices and experiences

---

[1] None of the women we interviewed identified themselves as lesbian; thus we are not able to discuss the particular experience of lesbian junior faculty. However, lesbian existences in the tenure track have been provided in other works (e.g., Bensimon 1992; Bronstein, Rothblum and Solomon 1993).

discussed in chapter 3. Ninety-nine junior faculty women were interviewed for this project. We are cognizant of the importance of differentiating among women on the basis of race, social class, and sexual orientation, and shall specify racial or ethnic identities when doing so does not violate our pledge of confidentiality. Further, this chapter is based largely on interviews with white women for several reasons: (1) the number of nonwhite U.S. women interviewed is very small and (2) gender and race or gender and ethnicity are not inseparable, so in those cases when these women spoke from the standpoint of their racial or ethnic identities we included them in the next chapter, which is on racial and ethnic faculty in predominantly white institutions.

Socialization as a Gendered Practice

Typically, socialization is understood as the initiation of prospective members into the culture of the institution, department, and profession. It is represented as a rite of passage that begins with probationary membership in the department and concludes, if one is successful, with the granting of lifetime tenure or, if unsuccessful, with immediate termination.

Women's Initiation

Preparing for a candidate's campus visit is not simply a matter of scheduling a series of meetings, announcing the candidate's "job talk," and arranging a real-estate tour. Just as the institution is looking the candidate over, the candidate is also forming impressions that will influence what offer she will accept, as well as her attitude toward prospective colleagues.

A feminist scholar being interviewed for a gender-studies position in a predominantly male department in one of the traditional disciplines described her interview as follows:

> We were having dinner and this one guy, he just kind of laughed and said 'Well, I think it is some kind of a joke . . . I don't know why we are doing this [looking to hire a feminist scholar].' All through the evening he expressed amusement by the efforts of marginalized people to try to position themselves within organizations and institutions where they don't really have the right to be.

Eventually the chair of the department apologized to the candidate and made it clear that they were truly interested in her. She was able to get over her anger and continue with the interview. When the position was offered, she accepted it. However, the treatment she received might have been a preview of the obstacles that could arise during her review for tenure and promotion. As a safeguard, she accepted the position with the condition that a faculty member from Women's Studies would be included in the department's review committee.

This white woman accepted the offer because she had no other job possibilities at the time; but had she received an offer from a department more hospitable to women and feminist scholarship in an equally prestigious institution, she probably would have taken it.

Off-putting interviews were uncommon; for the most part women spoke positively about their interviews. Still, most of the institutions we visited did not have guidelines that dealt specifically with the concerns of female candidates. To reiterate a point made in the previous chapter, the purpose of these vignettes is to portray specific problems that different individuals discussed. A thoughtful response ought not to be relief that such instances have not happened on one's own campus, but rather, proactive planning to ensure that they do not occur in the future. Our point is not that one institution is good and another bad, but that gendered relations are a fact of life. If we are to deal with such differences successfully, we must face them more forthrightly than we have done in the past.

Only one academic administrator had promulgated recruitment practices that spoke directly to the concerns of women and minorities. Starting from the premise that "the relationship the department develops with this person begins at the interview process and it has to start positively," this administrator established recruitment approaches centered on gender and race such as the following:

- Using language and graphics in job announcements that stressed the value of interdisciplinary scholarship and working and living in a multicultural community;
- Placing position announcements in specialized publications such as the *Women's Review of Books*;
- Ending the custom of interviewing candidates in hotel bedrooms at the site of disciplinary conferences (e.g., MLA, ASA);
- Organizing at least one lunch or one dinner for the candidate with people like themselves in order to get a frank assessment of the community. If it was a woman, then it was an all-women's lunch or dinner. If it was a minority person, it was a lunch or dinner with people from their ethnic, racial, or cultural background.

The institutions in our study were conscious of affirmative action and targeting recruitment efforts toward women and minorities. However, beyond recruiting women and minority applicants, there was not much evi-

dence that practices had been modified to avert gender- or race-based inequities at the point of hiring. For example, the custom of individual salary
negotiations has been shown to place women at a disadvantage, particularly
those who had not been mentored as graduate students and instructed on
negotiation rituals and courtship customs that are common in hiring practices
in the academy. Women often receive starting salaries that are lower than
those of their male peers because they don't know what to ask for or how to
negotiate. A white woman at a research university told us, "I didn't think
about negotiating. I felt lucky that I was getting a tenure-track job. I wanted
to say to the chair, 'I am really happy to come and I want the job, and you
have really been nice', and bring it to a closure."

As luck would have it, this woman ended up with a very good salary as
well as other benefits she did not think to ask for: a travel budget for her
research, a computer, and reimbursement for moving expenses. Had she
gone to another institution or even to a different department in the same
university, she probably would not have done as well. She was fortunate in
having been appointed to an academic unit led by an administrator who had
a policy of providing all new faculty members with substantially the same
salaries, research budgets, and travel allowances. Speaking about the policy,
the administrator who initiated it said,

> I told the department heads that women cannot bargain as aggressively as men.
> I told them, "I don't care whether they bargain or not." Just because a man
> says he needs a computer and the woman doesn't, that doesn't mean he gets
> the computer and she doesn't. If he gets a computer, she gets a computer. If
> she gets a research budget, he gets a research budget.

The woman who ended up with more than she asked for was a benefici-
ary of the new equity policy. She was hired at the same time as a Latino and
received a salary and benefits package that was practically the same as the
one he had bargained for himself. Had this policy not been in place she
probably would have started at a lower salary than that of her male colleague.

The problem with this practice, as well-intentioned as it is, is that it is
still disadvantageous for women: "Women can't play as well as men, so we
have to help them," rather than "The process is unfair so we have to eliminate bargaining." We should stress the latter.

Arriving on Campus: Women's First Impressions

The location, size, and furnishings of office space usually reflects one's status. More established faculty members get spacious, cheerful offices, and

probationary faculty get the small, somber cubicles. Different messages about power relations are conveyed by such decisions as who gets an office with a window, who has to make do with a used computer, who gets a new executive chair, and who gets wall-to-wall carpeting. A woman who walks into an office stocked with supplies, personalized cards, a working computer, and a functioning telephone gets a different message about the culture of the department than the one who learns on her first day that it will be six months before she is assigned an office.

The following are brief descriptions of the arrival experiences of five assistant professors, all of whom are newcomers in a very small institution.

White Male Newcomer #1:	I have been made to feel very welcome. When I ask for money, I get it. A few days after I arrived, the president called me to set up a meeting so we could get acquainted.
White Woman Newcomer #2:	I arrived to an empty department. No one was here. I was responsible for setting up my office. I had to figure out how to get my computer set up and in working order.
White Woman Newcomer #3:	It was totally chaotic. I did not get an office for months. I think it is inconceivable that they would have expected a man to function without an office.
White Woman Newcomer #4:	Well, I didn't get my computer until I'd been here for five weeks, so I missed all of the events that were only announced on e-mail.
African-American Woman Newcomer #5:	I had to get my own keys, computer, telephone, stationery. I didn't know there was a mailroom, and I just only got the key for it [more than a month after she arrived].

What impressions might one form based on the experiences of these new faculty members? A superficial interpretation is that the women's bad experiences compared to the man's good one suggest that structure accords privileges to men and places women at a disadvantage. However, the opening vignette in the previous chapter shows a white man whose initial campus experiences were as unwelcoming as those of the four women, suggesting that anyone, regardless of sex or race, may have a negative initial campus experience.

Our purpose is not to portray this institution as a bad place for women (in fact, the general consensus among the women interviewed was that it was a good place), or to document a systematic pattern of gender and race bias. Rather, by juxtaposing the experiences of these five professors, we want to show that the problem is not one of overt sexism or discrimination but rather that unwelcoming climates are created by unconscious actions that take on gendered meanings. From a gender perspective, the five vignettes could be interpreted as reflecting sex role stereotypes, e.g., "Men need to be cared for" and "Women know how to make do on their own."

Clearly, no one planned to treat the women differently from the man, it just worked out that way. The women's less-than-warm receptions were accidents of circumstance; nevertheless, it is important for members of an institution or department to reflect on the cumulative effect of such incidents on the climate for women. Unfortunately, we tend to dismiss such incidents as one-time occurrences or degender them with rational explanations: for example "The man was a star in his field," and that is why he was treated differently; "Woman #2's chair took time off for a vacation and forgot to order her computer"; "Woman #3 had the misfortune of being a casualty in an interdepartmental feud over office space"; "Woman #4 wanted a highly specialized computer that was delayed at the manufacturer"; and "Woman #5's department chair had a reputation for not being very thoughtful."

We do not contend that the pattern of gender discrimination suggested by the five vignettes is the result of overt sexist practices or from intentional acts of hostility. Without a doubt, lack of administrative acumen is certainly a major cause for the poorly planned receptions of new faculty. Furthermore, we believe that patterns of organization that place women at a disadvantage or reinforce their status as the "other" are produced by the absence of gender consciousness in the minds of decision-makers and its invisibility in the cultures of departments and institutions, as well as in the structures of tenure and promotion. Blindness to gender and gender relations in the construction of meaning prevents academic leaders, men and women, from discerning the multiple "readings" of institutional life. The challenge, then, is to consider how a female assistant professor in an all-male department might be inclined to "read" lack of planning for her arrival as a form of sexism. That is, individuals who have the power and authority to influence institutional functioning have to be adept at using gender as the lens through which they discern their institution's structures, practices, and culture.

Only Woman #3 raised the possibility of gender bias: "It is inconceivable that they would have expected a man to function without an office."

The other women did not suspect discrimination based on sex. Yes, they complained about the lack of forethought and preparation for their arrival, and they were generally annoyed, but they did not view themselves as victims of discrimination stemming from a masculinist culture. Rather, they felt very positive about the institution and attributed the lack of preparation for their arrival to external circumstances: lack of space, lack of clerical assistance, overworked administrators, etc. The minority woman, however, pointed out, "If this had been my first job, I would probably have taken things like the office and the computer as personal—you know, that they didn't think I was very important." A white woman with previous experience said that if this had been her first job she would have felt "vulnerable" and "lost."

In another institution sex stereotyping became obvious in the assignation of advisees. A white woman professor in the sciences who was the only one in her program said, "It's almost like they are on automatic pilot. If it's a woman, they assign her to me, or the women come to me, because they've been assigned to somebody else, and they say: 'I don't know what he's talking about, so could I have you for an advisor?'" When we asked this woman what the chair would do if she asked him to reduce her advisement load, she responded: "I think he would be quite willing to do that for me, if I asked . . . but I would feel like I am abandoning them [women students]."

Joining the Professoriate

Virginia Woolf's essay, *Three Guineas*, moves us to ask, "On what terms shall women join the professoriate?" What must women do to be accepted by the tenured faculty? The comments that follow reveal the pressures imposed on women who join male-dominated cultures:

> They are kind of patronizing, but I don't think they will try to hurt us [the junior faculty]. I am not worried about that, but I just feel that it is a kind of burden to get along with them all of the time. The main thing is just getting along with the guy colleagues . . . sometimes I feel uncomfortable, personally, with them. (Asian-American woman)

> I smile. I am nice. I try to always feel like I am in a good humor and that I am not challenging anyone, but especially I smile, and it drives me nuts sometimes. If I did not smile or had the personality of some of my [male] colleagues I would be out on my ear. The men can get away with being nerds, but there is no way I could get away with that, even if I wasn't doing feminist things. (White woman)

These passages are taken from interviews with two women, one an Asian American and the other white. Both are assistant professors at the same institution but in different departments. Although they are in different disciplines and in buildings at opposite ends of a sprawling campus, they have developed similar strategies to fit in. They engage in what we call "smile work" tactics to get along in departments dominated by senior male colleagues.

Doing "Smile Work"

"Smile work" takes many different forms, but basically it is a culturally imposed strategy women use to fit into departments with a tradition of male dominance. Sometimes these are departments in which the faculty have not internalized the need to be more diverse and have hired women and/or minorities because of external pressures to comply with affirmative action goals. Typically, they tend to think of equal opportunity as "adding women" without reconsidering socialization practices in order to be more welcoming. Male-dominated cultures encourage feminine stereotypical behaviors that make women appear "unobjectionable," congenial and cheerful rather than strident and unpredictable.

At a small college, a senior male professor reminisced about the "patriarchal" ways of the past, lamenting that "the faculty club is no longer a place where the wives and children come on Friday nights." A white woman administrator at the same college said, "There is a substantial number of faculty who remember the time when they were masters of the universe . . . and they are still living in that culture." A white man in a research university said of his department, "There is still a definite gender bias especially among the senior people. I think you're probably a couple of steps ahead if you are a white male around here, but that's probably just stating what people already know or stating the obvious." In institutions such as these, where the imprint of a patriarchal past is still quite discernible, women employ the behavioral and symbolic practices of "smile work" in conscious ways.

Smile work entails the symbolic management of behavior to present oneself as being pleasing and agreeable. An assistant professor in a difficult working relationship with a very powerful senior professor said,

> I accommodate him by backing out, by joking with him, by pretending that we get along and that I don't mind hearing about his sex life.

On the surface, she behaves like a good-natured colleague, a "team player," one of the guys. The act of accommodation inherent in smile work can be costly, a fact she admitted the very moment we entered her office.

Before getting started with the interview, she said, "I am so glad you are here . . . I have no one to talk with about these things." She then told us of her decision to move to another institution:

> As long as I remain here, I feel I will never be able to establish my own identity. He [senior colleague] makes me feel like a glorified graduate student, and it is very hard on my self-esteem . . . but I cannot afford to have him as my enemy at tenure time. I have to live with this situation.

What this individual has to do in order to survive and succeed involves identity, not "only" adaptation. A man has to learn the code, but that doesn't necessarily mean that he has to conceal who he is, whereas a woman in this situation may be obliged to falsify herself to a greater extent. The point is not to say that men have it easier, but that the same "problem" must be interpreted in a variety of ways.

Women who felt pressured into being accommodating spoke about feelings of powerlessness, loss of self, and lack of self-confidence. A feminist scholar complained that a senior professor treated her as if she were "his personal property." "He wanted to boss me, introduce me around as if I were his protege," she said. She resented the subordinating gestures of her colleague and would have liked to bring them to his attention. However, she received a negative mid-tenure review, and "rather than making a big thing out of it," she said, "I was advised to try to win over one of the professors who voted against me . . . so I am trying to win this person over, using regular, you know, normal ways." Then she added the caveat: "I want to have positive evaluations, but I am not going to lose my dignity."

In a hierarchical and status-conscious structure, the dualism of "senior" versus "junior" underscores differences in power, knowledge, and prestige that characterize relationships between experts and novices. Indeed, at one institution we visited, the participants had replaced the term "junior faculty" with one they felt was less objectionable and power-laden—"probationary faculty." The status of novice is full of contradictions, uncertainties and anxieties about one's worth. For women in predominantly male departments, the difficulties are intensified by the combined politics of tenure and promotion and gender relations. A Latina told us, "I have to demonstrate I am humble and malleable" in order to succeed. An Asian woman described a faculty meeting with new graduate students that was "dominated by one of the senior men. . . . When my turn to speak came, I mentioned that I do traditional things and that I also teach courses on feminist topics. I made it known that I have several interests. Immediately after I said that, he warned the graduate students to be focused in one area. I felt he was undermining me because I did not just do traditional stuff."

One cannot know for sure whether the senior professor's remarks were triggered by her comments, and if they were, whether their intended meaning was as she interpreted it. However, in an environment where outstanding graduate students can enhance professors' status and prestige, the professor's admonition "to focus" took on a derogatory meaning. The comment emphasized the woman's junior status, which she feared would make her appear as inexperienced and therefore not necessarily a prime choice to serve as dissertation advisor for doctoral students.

Doing "Mom Work"

Another form of accommodation that women engaged in was "mom work," a term used by an assistant professor to describe the imposition of nurturing and caretaking roles on women. Just as some department cultures fostered "smile work," others promulgated the stereotype of the nurturing woman. The pressure to perform "mom work" was greatest in small private colleges. These are colleges with a greater-than-usual dependency on tuition revenues and where there is an unstated expectation for faculty to be popular with students and their parents.

According to one white woman, the pressure to be popular with students was "amplified for female professors." "It's a personality issue. You have to, you know, be extroverted and be willing to disclose personal issues, personal information; they [students] definitely look for some personal information." A gay white man said, "I team-taught a class with a woman, and some of the comments in the evaluations were surprising . . . they said she giggled like an adolescent, and I didn't perceive her like that at all. . . . she joked the way male professors often do, and the students shot her down because she is a woman." He also remarked that students "tend to cling to women professors, and when they are not allowed to cling, when the female professor tries to make her own time, she's considered selfish, whereas with the male professor, it's like he has more important things to do." In the same vein, a white woman made this observation:

> We are expected to be more nurturing, more forgiving, more disclosing. Being forgiving is very important. Forgiving students for not meeting a deadline, for not being able to find a printer or typewriter, or because athletics or jobs interfere with coming to class. There is a whole lot of forgiving to do.

In response to a reprimand provoked by a student's complaint, a white woman said:

> I got a letter from the faculty personnel committee saying that "we hope that you make yourself available to students." So I had to respond. I showed them

that I had set aside six hours a week for office hours and that I gave students my home phone number as well as my office number.

Another white woman observed:

We are expected to be good teachers, and when a man does a good job teaching, he gets complimented. When a man in the department is a nurturing father, he is seen as caring, and when a woman runs around taking care of her kids, it's seen as that she's simply doing her role, or worse, as interfering with her work.

A woman faculty member attributed her difficulties with male students to the college's "informal culture," in which males felt free to be more aggressive. She said:

I had males, typically sitting at the back of the room, who seemed to make it a point of challenging me, getting me on an issue to the point where, for some reason, it appeared to be a way of testing me, or playing out some power struggle.

However, a colleague of hers disagreed:

I think there are other factors that contribute to it, too, besides the informality. I think the student population at this college is less diverse in terms of economic and cultural background than you would find in other schools, for example at a community college. The students feel a camaraderie that lets them exhibit "machismo"; they have permission from each other to do that. A lot of times it comes from the male athletes, and I am not sure our P.E. faculty is doing enough to tell the male athletes that that's not acceptable.

One white woman said, "I would not go to senior faculty members with this problem because I don't know how they would react." Instead, she says, "I start questioning them [the male students], I move over, I'm standing, they're sitting, you know, I make a real blatant power move on these guys. I stand right next to them, and I start calling on them, by name, and asking them questions, and if they're not prepared, which frequently happens to be the case, that pretty much takes care of the situation."

Not all women, however, know how to use confrontation to affirm their authority, nor should they have to. This is not an isolated teaching problem experienced by some female faculty. Rather, it is a problem that arises from an institution's culture, and as such, it needs to be addressed at the institutional level. As one of these women pointed out ". . . this is a gender issue, and I think the men's sports coaches can say we've had enough of this, we want a different culture . . . but they are not saying that. They say, 'Oh well, that's just the jocks, and jocks will be jocks.' . . . You know, it's a variation of 'boys will be boys.' "

Pressure to do "mom work" was also obvious from how frequently female faculty members were enlisted into doing more than a fair share of a department's domestic-type work. A white woman spoke about agreeing to teach a required freshman seminar for the third consecutive year even though the department had a policy that no one should have to teach it for more than two years. She said,

> They have to twist arms to get people to teach the required freshman seminar. The chair was in a bind, and when he said, "Could you think about doing it another year?" I said, "Sure" because it is fun to teach.

The catch was that the professor who teaches the seminar also becomes the advisor of that year's freshman cohort. After three years, this professor's advisement load had grown to approximately 60 students, about 10 times the advising loads of the tenured faculty.

Studies of women in academe (Aisenberg and Harrington 1988; Turner and Thompson 1993; Clark and Corcoran, 1986) report that female graduate students and beginning faculty are frequently not part of professional and social circles in which newcomers learn about the nonacademic aspects of being a professor, such as how to negotiate one's salary, travel funds, release time, and equipment. Similarly, studies report that when women enter the academy as tenure-track faculty, they often remain outside the social and professional networks and therefore they are less likely to know the unstated criteria that senior faculty use in making decisions about tenure and promotion. Faculty who lack the strategic knowledge necessary for making informed choices end up like the professor above, accepting extra "domestic" work only to realize later (and sometimes too late) that it has very little value as a criterion for promotion and tenure. The professor who volunteered to teach the freshman seminar for the third consecutive year now regretted having done so:

> I really shouldn't have been teaching the first year seminar. I thought at the time it would be a wonderful course to teach, and it will be a big plus in the service department. Well, service you can just about write off, if you do anything in the way of service, it will be ok. I should have just protected my time, and said: "I haven't got time to do this and still do a lot of scholarly stuff. Find somebody else." But the department chair was desperate for somebody to do it, and when I said, "Sure," I wasn't thinking that it would be more negative than positive.

This professor blames herself for not having been more assertive. But what about the department chair? Shouldn't he have known better? How fair was it for the chair, given his position of authority, to make her choose between helping him out or appearing uncooperative? Clearly, the chair did not intend to overburden the professor. Nevertheless, he overburdened her because he failed to recognize the appearance of there being a choice. The professor could have said yes, or she could have said no. In a power relationship this is not a choice that can be freely exercised.

Similarly, we do not agree with the position taken by a provost at a research university who told us, "One thing that I tell them [women and minority faculty] is that saying 'no' in itself may be a good thing. If the department head says 'How would you like to teach the 100-level introductory course?' and they say, 'No,' then that sends a message to the department head that this person is really committed to working with graduate students and doing research." While this is certainly good advice on how to survive and succeed in a research-oriented culture, it places the onus for being socialized on the untenured woman. Also, it is possible that a white man's refusal to teach introductory-level undergraduate courses may be more acceptable than the same response from a woman. His refusal conforms to the stereotypical male script, i.e., teaching interferes with his research, but her refusal departs from the stereotypical female script, i.e., she is not acquiescent.

Ideally, junior faculty should be able to rely on their chairs for support, advice, and mentoring, and it is therefore unfair and thoughtless to make requests that junior faculty may feel they cannot refuse. A woman faced with this very predicament said,

> I tried very hard to not succumb to what felt like a lot of pressure to participate [in committees] from my chair. I'm trying to establish myself as a part of the community here, and if I, you know, back up and say, "Wait a minute! The rules say you can't make me do this," what kind of image am I painting of myself? And, you know, it is important to be accepted by my colleagues, and that's quite a bit of pressure.

The culture of the department structures the behaviors, choices, and self-presentation of junior faculty. A woman with more than three years on the tenure track told us that she would advise a newly appointed assistant professor "to play the academic strategy game: Take time away from teaching and don't be available for committee work." Ironically, she admitted that she had not followed her own advice: "I haven't done that because I get a lot of my human needs met by teaching and servicing." The point is that in a departmental culture structured according to the preferences of the male faculty, women may view service activities that take them away from research and writing as opportunities to establish relationships outside their departments. Department chairs who may be in favor of more diverse hiring do not realize that faculty members who are one-of-a-kind often have difficulty in dealing with alienating departmental cultures. Spending time with students, devoting themselves to teaching, and volunteering for service rather than representing what women are naturally predisposed to do well may be nothing more than opportunities for connecting with others and forming relationships. Department chairs who understand this can take measures to help female faculty members to establish social and professional networks.

Women and Collegiality

Being included as a colleague was a persistent concern for many women. One white woman said,

> I have zero collegiality in my department. They don't know what I do. I feel alienated, not on an equal footing with the men. Sometimes I have lunch in the faculty club and see the guys from my department eating together. In the three years I have been here, no one has asked me to have lunch.

In contrast, another white woman in the same department (different subspecialty) said the opposite about her colleagues:

> It is a very congenial group. Most of us have lunch together almost every day. We know where to look for each other. Even though I am the only woman, I always feel I can go over.

Needless to say, there could be any number of reasons for one woman feeling left out of the collegial circle and another feeling included. Perhaps one is more extroverted than the other; perhaps the first woman's colleagues have not realized that the socialization of newcomers is their responsibility. We noted in the previous chapter that one woman thought men did not "invite" others for lunch, so she behaved just like the men, whereas another woman commented that she had never been asked to lunch. The woman who saw herself as being part of the inside group felt that her colleagues were familiar with her work. In contrast, the woman who felt excluded from the men's circle declared, "They don't know what I do."

Collegiality is far more likely to occur when there is a shared orientation to the discipline. For example, the woman who felt included by her male colleagues mentioned that a Marxist or a feminist would probably disrupt the group's harmony. Additionally, the unspoken rules of collegiality meant that she had to put up with "backlash" humor. She said,

> There is a professor who jokes about white men not being able to get jobs . . . he says it jokingly, but you can tell he has serious feelings about it. . . . I think he accepts me now, but he was one of the senior faculty who did not want me here. . . . No one says anything to him . . . they shrug it off; they say, "That is just the way he is."

In contrast, a white woman with a distinctively different approach to her discipline and teaching found herself

> getting slammed [by colleagues] for being ideological and political in the classroom. They said my teaching could be supplemented by more authority-centered criticism, meaning that instead of allowing student voices, I should lecture. It rankled me. I was angry. I thought they would respect my work.

Senior women, particularly if they were the only female full professor, were not necessarily any more responsive to junior females than were the senior men. For example, a white junior woman said of a senior colleague, "I have asked her to have lunch, but she is very overworked and has not responded."

Women in the Sciences and Engineering

Women in mathematics and the sciences who were often the "only woman" spoke about their loneliness. Asked what it is like to be a female professor, a white woman said, "In the math department, it's a very lonely experience. . . . Math is a very male subject . . . the expectation of how a mathematician thinks, or how a mathematician operates are very masculine expectations. A lot of mathematicians tend to be very aggressive people, very argumentative . . . and that is not my personality at all. . . . part of it is just me, but I think in general female mathematicians tend to be not nearly so argumentative as the males . . . so I find it very difficult to operate in that sort of environment, it is very hard to handle."

Women in male-identified fields often sensed a lack of respect or interest from their colleagues and felt marginalized. This mathematician said,

> It makes me question how valuable I am, because I always have this sense that I should be different from how I am. And I find it very oppressive, I have a feeling that I am always kind of struggling to justify myself. I always feel that I somehow am not . . . I have to work to gain their respect . . . and, I don't want to have to think that much about it, I want to just be able to go about my

activities, to do my teaching, to learn, you know, new kinds of scholarly stuff, and instead I have to worry about all those other issues, and it takes a lot of energy.

A colleague in the sciences, also a white woman, agreed: "I also find it very lonely, even though two out of the five faculty in my department are women." She described the difference between the sciences and liberal arts as follows: "I have a sense that there is a much tighter and more supportive group of women who are in the humanities and social sciences departments. They're all in the same building, it's easier to run into people, it's easier to make connections with people."

Both the mathematician and the scientist were assigned service responsibilities that fit the category of "mom work." As one put it, she was asked to do "things that are kind of peripheral to both teaching and scholarship." One was the editor of the department's newsletter and the other was the advisor for all pre-med students, which entailed "a lot of administrative work related to providing support for students applying to medical schools." She said, "I do a lot of public relations, I meet with the parents, and I go and talk to groups of new students."

Structured Absences: The Sexless Professorial Body

"I am a little self-conscious about being the professor with a child," said a white woman. An Asian-American recalled, "I felt uncomfortable mentioning that I had a child or that I had a relatively newborn baby at the time of the interview. I had gone on another job interview at the time I was eight months pregnant, and when the faculty saw I was expecting, they looked shocked . . . them seeing me as a pregnant woman was an immediate negative reaction. Once they found out I was pregnant, their attitudes toward me changed." A third woman admitted, "I felt that if my child was sick, I'd be too embarrassed to miss class . . . no one else has a family, so I felt some tension about having kids."

At another institution, individuals commented that when a man had a child, "it was a moment for celebration, but when a woman had a child she heard comments such as, 'I hope this doesn't jeopardize tenure.'" One woman who had a child when she arrived in her department recalled that everyone was understanding; "but when I had my second child, it was clear that I'd made a mistake. 'Don't you know about birth control?' someone actually said." Another person in the institution remarked that when this individual brought her infant to the college, the male faculty disapproved of how the department had become a "daycare center." In contrast, at a small college, a woman said, "I have two young kids who manage to get sick at the beginning of every semester I've taught, and I don't get any grief when I teach my class and run right home. . . . I assume that it's not specific to me, it's just a flexible kind of place that acknowledges that people have lives outside of the institution." And she added, "It made *all* of me feel welcome, not just the part that the institution was going to get a benefit out of."

Before affirmative action and women's entry into the academy the professorial image was that of the "academic man"; when we spoke about a college professor, the image conjured up was masculine and we always used "he" when speaking about an unspecified professor. Nowadays we talk about faculty as if they are an undifferentiated class of people, disembodied and sexless. This generalized image of faculty makes some women professors with children feel aberrant. "Structuring absence" is the term used by a male professor to describe the academy's "muteness about personal lives." He said,

> It is symptomatic of a structuring absence . . . just as other things are there because they're structured, this one is deliberately unspoken. Things are formed around that, people don't talk about the difficulties of their home life because they're not supposed to. It's not gallant, it's not jock enough, it's not steroid enough.

The "structured absence" of the personal sphere creates disadvantages for women with children that most institutions are not addressing adequately. Institutionally sponsored day care services are rare. Even though some institutions made provisions for stopping the tenure clock for women who gave birth, none had paid maternity leaves that were longer than a few weeks. The lack of paid maternity leave policies left it to the discretion of department chairs and their willingness to circumvent regulations in order to grant semester-long leaves to female faculty members with a newborn child. One professor said "the chair was supportive once he found out a precedent had been set, but he did not initiate anything." A Latina in a commuting marriage said, "In this university, everything seems to happen at the department level, and your chair can make your life miserable." Fortunately, her department chair was unusually understanding and sensitive about the personal lives of faculty. He told us, "Smart people tend to marry smart people," and went on to say:

> I have one woman whose husband is a foreign service officer stationed in another country, so they commute. I have another whose husband is involved in a job that takes him all over the world without much notice. These are strains that did not exist to the same degree 10 or 15 years ago, and we have

not figured out how to accommodate them in the process of promotion and tenure.

He also observed,

> We have a pregnancy leave policy, and if a faculty member is adversely affected by a pregnancy they could stop the tenure clock for one year. It made great sense. Guess who took advantage of it the most—male faculty members even though their productivity may not be as adversely affected as that of their wives.

Sometimes long-term leaves could be managed only if other members of the faculty were willing to cover for the absent professor. This arrangement was neither fair to the colleagues who assumed the extra work nor to the women who became dependent on and indebted to the kindness of others. For example, the male professor who said, "My colleague, she managed to get pregnant so she would deliver in the middle of the school year," was obviously annoyed. Clearly it is unrealistic to expect women faculty to schedule the time of conception so that childbirth coincides with the slow season in academia. It is also unrealistic for institutions not to have provisions that protect professors who also happen to be women and mothers.

None of the women were bitter or angry about the impact this "structuring absence" had on them. Quite to the contrary, they were grateful for the kindness and understanding of their department chairs. One woman said, "He went to bat for me and got me a medical leave so I got paid anyway." Another woman said, "The chair of my department has been real supportive of me. When I had my baby, he *allowed* me to not teach for a semester. I had six months off, and I was able to stay home with my son. It is not a university policy, it is just something he did to try and help me."

A minority woman who was herself directly affected was moved to work on the institutionalization of paid maternity leaves. She said, "Right now it is very individualized, and some departments have been very hostile to pregnant women who approach the chair and ask not even for a leave but just a lighter teaching load."

While all the institutions in the study have made progress in terms of hiring women faculty and bridging the gender gap, the culture of the institutions and departments in some critical ways still operates according to norms from a time when the prototypical professor was a white male whose wife stayed home and took care of their children. Indeed, the lack of paid maternity leave policies accentuates women's difference from the norm. Lack of paid maternity leave policies disempowers women because it forces them to dependent on and be indebted to the goodwill of individuals whose support they need to succeed as academics.

Characteristics of Women-Affirming Cultures

Up to this point, we have concentrated on the cultural barriers women must overcome to establish themselves and be accepted in male-identified academic milieus. The academic cultures we have described seem more indifferent to women than openly contemptuous of them, more likely to exhibit institutionalized rather than overt sexism. Feminist scholars have called attention to the "invisible paradigms" (Shuster & VanDyne, 1984), the "communal unconscious" (Aiken et al., 1987) that structures departmental and institutional cultures that pose barriers to the integration of women faculty. As we have already mentioned, we heard few reports of egregious sex discrimination or sex harassment. Women expressed discomfort, annoyance, and frustration with male dominance that permeated their departments and institutions, but none described her situation as so horribly oppressive as to be intolerable. None of the women said they planned to give up their plans for an academic career; none expressed regrets about having chosen the professoriate as their vocation.

By the same token, few of the women described their departments or institutions as being totally affirming for women, and a relatively small number described department or institutional characteristics that made them good for women. Among the factors that women identified as contributing to a positive climate were chairs who were sensitive to the personal lives of women, an equity-oriented institutional ethos, and a critical mass of women. One said:

> In this department being a woman is great. We have a lot of them. Of the five junior faculty, three are women. My colleagues treat me as though they think I am smart and that I am worthy of consideration when we are debating.

Agreeing with her colleague, the second woman said:

> They have done a very nice job of recruiting women, so I would say, for the most part, there aren't a lot of gender issues. I have not ever been treated in a condescending manner. I have no sense that women are treated as second-class citizens and that our work is not taken seriously. . . . We are not shoved off to marginal or minor committees. . . . The year I came in, they hired five faculty; three of those were filled with women.

These two women have been appointed to a newly created multi-disciplinary department in which junior faculty outnumber senior faculty. The youthfulness of the department along with its multidisciplinary mission create an ethos that values diversity.

However, it also helped that the ideological orientation of these two women was congruent with mainstream theories and research methods. For example, one professor, although interested in issues of social inequality, was nevertheless a mainstream quantitative researcher. She said,

> If I would have been more radical, more of an activist, I suspect that it would have been more difficult. This department is mainstream enough that I would have really had to be on my toes to rise above the kinds of critiques that everybody was going to come ready to launch at me.

The other woman observed, "If I was a deconstructionist feminist, it wouldn't play very well at all, but I can't imagine them hiring anyone quite that radical. I would say that if it's relatively mainstream feminist types of issues, it would not be problematic."

Finally, the department chair was pivotal in creating the climate that made these women feel recognized and respected as professionals. The Latina said,

> He always encourages me to show him my work. He is very complimentary . . . when my teaching evaluations come back and they are positive, he comes in and he tells me. He is not guarded in his praise. He is very complimentary of my performance.

She also praised him for his sensitivity to unique personal circumstances. She said,

> My husband and I commute, and the chair has been very understanding when I have had to leave on a Friday to go spend a long weekend with my husband. He treats me like a professional . . . as long as I do my work he lets the reins loose. . . . He lets me arrange things however it accommodates me best.

At a different institution, a woman from the Middle East described her chair as thoughtful, sensitive, and "wonderful." She said, "We talk all the time. Not only was my office completely set up when I arrived, but he knew that my husband needs to finish his dissertation, so he gave me an extra key to my office and put another big table in there for him so he could work there, too."

Along with leadership, institutional mission can be a powerful influence on the culture of an institution. A woman who left a large research-oriented university for a small teaching-oriented college with a strong commitment to a multicultural mission said that the difference between the two places was "startling" and that she "couldn't have looked for an institution that would have been the complete opposite [of research university] any more closely than this college." She said,

> When I arrived, the woman who runs the computer center offered me anything that I needed. The dean has always said, "Please stop by and talk to me," as has the president of the college, and it's genuine. You can tell they would welcome you to stop and chat with them, and tell them how things are going.

She also commented on being

> quite surprised at the number of females that are in administrative positions with power, and not just figurehead sorts of positions. I haven't noticed any blatant sexism. . . . I feel I have been respected by everybody that I have come in contact with.

She concluded by saying, "I feel like I'm waiting for the other shoe to drop. You know, that this can't be reality."

A critical mass of women also contributes to the creation of affirming climates for women. A white woman who had done her graduate work at a prestigious northeast university and started her career in a small college said, "Having been in a university environment that was incredibly hostile to women, coming here seems like heaven. There are a lot of women senior faculty. In the university, there was only one in the department, and she was very token." A white professor of economics in a department where three of the six faculty members are women said, "It is very unusual; in other colleges I would have been the token female. Here they weren't looking for a woman because they didn't need to fill any gender gap." Being among other women meant not having the feeling "constantly that you have to join a men's club." A European Latina said, "It makes a difference. In the university I came from, women were marginalized . . . here whenever we want to bring a speaker, we bring a feminist. . . . All the senior women in the department are in the key university committees where important decisions get made."

Even though department chairs, deans, and vice presidents spoke about affirmative action and efforts to recruit women, almost none of these academic leaders stated that the dismantling of institutionalized forms of sexism was one of their priorities. The reason was not that they did not care, rather the state of "communal unconscious" that develops from the internalization of the "invisible paradigms" that structure the culture of the academy and the disciplines prevents senior faculty and administrators from seeing how their very practices might create and reproduce institutionalized forms of sexism. In other words, it is possible for academic leaders to target recruitment efforts toward women and minorities without giving much thought to transforming male-identified departmental cultures. The meritocratic discourse of promotion and tenure is effective camouflage for the gendered aspects of seemingly neutral practices. As a consequence, individuals in positions of authority, power, and influence construe affirmative action as a matter of "adding women" to a presumably gender-neutral structure. Just as feminist scholars have pointed out that making the curriculum more inclusive is not simply a matter of adding women to syllabi but rather demands the "deconstruction and reconstruction" of the disciplines in order to be truly transformative, the same can be said about the integration of women into the professoriate.

The one exception to the "add women" approach was a dean and feminist scholar who was willing to discard recruitment, hiring, and evaluation practices that undermine the achievement of integrating the academy. She said,

> When I walked in the door there were three lawsuits in process: two by minority women and one by an Anglo [sic] woman in different departments charging the institution with discrimination not only in the promotion and tenure process, but in the ways that they had been treated during their time here. I also found that we had a very poor record of hiring and retaining women in most of the departments and that the most serious problems were at the senior levels where there were simply no women in most departments.

Thus she changed position announcements to appeal more directly to women and minority applicants:

> We changed our advertisements . . . the way in which we physically presented ourselves in advertisements, we talked about what it is to be a multicultural community. I then had all the faculty who were going to be on interview committees meet with the affirmative action officer. We put our advertisements in places that they have never been before, like the *Women's Review of Books*.

Furthermore, faculty search procedures were structured to increase the likelihood of women and minority candidates:

> The first year, I said to the committees that all the searches would be affirmative action. I told them "You are going to have two piles. One pile is white

males and the other pile is minorities and women. Only if you cannot find a viable candidate in the pile of minorities and women can you go to the white male pile."

Additionally, women and minorities were well represented in faculty search committees but were also protected from being overburdened:

I said, "From hence forward all search committees will be gender balanced with an equal number of males and females and one-third minority representation." Needless to say, we did not have enough minorities or women in each department to make up committees, so we borrowed them from department to department. But that meant some women and some minority faculty were being tediously borrowed. So, I said to department heads, "Any faculty member who is being borrowed has got to have course relief." I gave this faculty one course relief and used them to develop the search committees.

Search committees were less likely to dismiss candidates whose work did not conform to normative concepts of scientific research because "they were so differently composed that the applications were read differently."

These gender and race motivated interventions produced tangible results:

We got a very different cohort than we have gotten before. During my first years our hires were 70% women and about 30% were minorities. It doesn't mean I did not hire any white males. I did hire some white males.

To increase women's chances for success and retention, this dean invented a mentoring system that avoids placing the senior professors (most of whom are men) in the role of superior and the junior female faculty member in the role of subordinate. Instead of creating mentoring pairs, each newcomer was assigned three mentors: one male and one female, neither of whom are from the same department as the junior faculty member, and the third person is another junior faculty member. Newcomers are paired up with faculty mentors on the basis of non-academic interests, mainly to encourage professors to establish some common ground through shared interests (e.g., hobbies, sports, children, etc.). The hoped-for outcome is that personal knowledge will break down ideological and generational barriers between senior and junior faculty. A woman who took part in this program said:

I was assigned three mentors. Two are full professors and the other one is an assistant professor. The dean mandates that one of the mentors be an assistant professor so that mentoring is not based on power relations. One of the mentors is a really wonderful super professor from another department who is interested in post-colonial stuff and that was good for me. The dean provides free lunches for the mentoring group twice a semester.

Women faculty praised the dean for her initiatives against what they perceived as gender-based inequities. One woman said, "She has done some extremely important work here as a feminist dean. . . . Her presence has made a big difference in the achievement of things like unofficial leaves for women who give birth and that we are now able to request a stoppage of the tenure clock when we give birth. This did not exist before her." However, she encountered considerable resistance from long-time faculty. One professor said, "She is a very strong feminist, and the faculty don't agree with her tactics."

Women-Centered Structures

Feminist administrators with the power to challenge institutionalized forms of sexism are rare in most colleges and universities. Women-centered academic structures, however, which are now more common, were mentioned repeatedly as places that alleviate the loneliness and alienation felt by female faculty members. Among the twelve institutions included in the study, all but one had a women's studies program.

For some women faculty, these academic programs were far more important in providing collegial support than their home departments. A feminist scholar in a very conservative, male-dominated department said, "If I get weirded out about what's going on here, I can call one of the faculty in women's studies and say I just need to talk about what's going on." Another said, "Once I got here, I found out that there is a really strong women's studies program with a wonderful director, and I found a lot of colleagues with whom I could exchange ideas." She added, "That makes a big difference in making the university seem attractive and deciding to remain here."

In a small liberal arts college, a female faculty member in a science department told us that she had just come from "the Feminist Seminar":

> We are a group of faculty who gets together once a month to discuss feminist scholarship. . . . I wouldn't make myself read Toni Morrison's new edited volume [*Race-ing Justice, En-gendering Power*] if there wasn't some motivation for doing so.

In addition to providing a place for intellectual development, the seminar provided her with personal support:

It's a way for me to connect with women senior faculty who are in some sense role models for me, as a new faculty person here.

A man who was doing research on "the celebration of the gladiator as the ultimate jock" said, "My male colleagues are cordial but they never ask about my work" and pointed out that he has found more support in a feminist faculty seminar.

We asked faculty members if their participation in a feminist seminar counted as scholarship or professional service. One professor said, "This is an extra. . . . We are doing important work . . . this year we are focusing on readings related to racism, and it is critical that faculty be involved in such discussions, but that's not acknowledged as a legitimate contribution to the academic atmosphere."

Women's academic groups are also responsible for much of the formal and informal mentoring that women receive. A woman mentioned, "A group of us started the women's faculty group when we were new here. We've had several programs on tenure and how to prepare for it, and on career plans and how to direct your writing and to organize your life so you can teach and write and be a person at the same time." After having attended a roundtable discussion organized by the women's faculty group, an assistant professor told us, "Women who have served on the tenure committee came to speak to us, and it was there that I learned that an edited volume doesn't count the same way as submitting my work to a specialized journal would. People would hear me give talks at conferences and would say, 'I'd like you to submit that to the book I'm editing.' If I had known earlier, I probably would have turned down some requests and done different kinds of writing on my own."

In presenting these stories, it is not our intent to concoct a composite profile of "the woman's experience in the tenure track." Rather, we have used them to illustrate the multiplicity of women's experiences and also to show that these experiences are shaped by the intersections of gender, race, ethnicity and culture (institutional and departmental).

The stories provide understandings of how some female faculty members, most of whom are white, enact their academic roles and how they respond to the cultures of their departments and institutions. The stories have a familiar ring in that they reiterate circumstances that have contributed to women leaving the academy before the tenure decision (Bronstein, Rothblum and Solomon 1993), publishing less than men (Astin and Davis 1985), taking longer than men to achieve tenure and promotions to associate or full professor (Bentley and Blackburn 1992), lacking characteristics associated with exemplary newcomers (Boice 1992), and to gravitate toward "intentional intellectual communities" (Gumport 1990) in search of academic and social support. In looking at these stories through the lenses of critical and feminist postmodernism, we extend previous analyses of the status of women academics from the individual level (e.g., behaviors, personality, attitudes) to the institutional level, thereby revealing cultural norms that pose a barrier to the socialization of women (Bronstein, Rothblum and Solomon 1993; Fox 1985). This suggests that the particular experience of a female junior professor is shaped not only by her individual behaviors but also, and perhaps more significantly, by gender and power relations that typify the culture of a department or institution. What this means is that from a critical and feminist postmodernist standpoint, we interpret "smile work" and "mom work" as behavioral patterns produced by male-identified academic cultures. That is to say, the problem is not that women suffer from work overload only because they have not figured out how to protect their time or because they do not know how to say "no" to the requests of others. Neither is the problem one of women doing more service work or more teaching because such work fulfills "women's needs" to feel useful, needed, and competent. Nor can we attribute it to being symptomatic of the "feminine version of the academic career pattern" (Dwyer, Flynn and Inman 1993). Rather, a critical and feminist postmodernist standpoint frames "mom work" as a cultural norm in settings that are predominantly male yet are not conscious of how this maleness structures the lives of female and male faculty members according to traditional gender roles. Additionally, the gender and power relations in academic settings can be so alienating that doing service might make women feel less invisible, less isolated, less lonely. A woman's sense of invisibility or isolation or loneliness is not simply a matter of developing a more outgoing personality. Institutional cultures also need to change seemingly innocent and natural practices that have the effect of placing women at a disadvantage and silencing them.

The experiences of professors in more women-affirming academic departments suggest that academic leaders can create organizational cultures that are responsive to gender differences. For example, department chairs who recognized the interdependence between the private and public lives of faculty and made accomodations for women's responsibilities in the private sphere created environments in which gender difference did not translate into an impairment or negative condition. The positive as well as the negative experiences reported by these women suggest that there are a variety of ways in which academic leaders can transform the cultures of their departments, schools, or institutions. For example, women spoke highly of department chairs who provided them with feedback about their work, were cognizant of their accomplishments, and acknowledged them. Seemingly innocuous comments from a department chair, such as "Your course evaluations came in and they are just great," or "Your presentation in the graduate seminar has sparked a lot of interest," or "I plan to use your article on . . . as one of the required readings for my class" are symbolic gestures of recognition, respect, and acceptance.

CHAPTER 5

Socialization and Cultural Taxation: Race and Ethnicity in the Academy

> I often get into disagreements with other faculty members when we discuss what kind of an individual we want and the strategies we should take to attract that individual. I strongly support getting minority candidates and doing whatever is necessary to attract them here, but some of my colleagues don't see it that way. They see it as favoritism. I see it as affirmative action.

In most colleges and universities, the whiteness of the professoriat stands out conspicuously, particularly in comparison to the more racially and ethnically diverse composition of the student body. Colleges and universities are increasingly more conscious of the need for a diverse professoriat. Both large and small institutions have established target-of-opportunity programs to encourage and reward departments that fill positions with members of U.S. racial and ethnic minority groups. The institutions in our study were also involved in efforts to recruit African-American, Hispanic, Asian-American and Native-American faculty. Just a few days before our visit, the president of a very small institution had made a statement urging the faculty "to be more diligent about the search for minority faculty." Approvingly, an African-American woman who was a newcomer to the institution told us, "He said all the right things and some of us said, 'Where did that come from?' It was a wonderful statement, and there was no precedent for it."

As one might expect, the degree of effort to increase the number of minority faculty members varied from institution to institution, and so did the outcomes. A very small and poor institution that had only one African-American professor in 1991 had hired six more by 1993. This institution's success was attributed to a trustee mandate declaring the hiring of minority faculty an institutional priority. The mandate was strictly enforced by the president and his academic administrators, primarily by taking an unusually bold step: aborting searches that concluded with an all-white short list. An African American who was recruited after having submitted her name to a national databank for minority faculty attributed her hiring to two reasons: the dean's insistence that people of color be appointed and, also, "because I really underplayed myself in the interview, I think the men felt they could fit me into their model. . . . I can be very inviting, very gentle, very non-threatening."

In large universities, there were varying levels of commitment to minority hiring within colleges and departments. The humanities and social sciences tended to be more conscious of and receptive to minority hiring efforts, and the sciences and business more insistent on hiring based on "objective, merit, and race-blind" criteria. The chair of an all-white business department, unhappy with the emphasis on hiring minority faculty, said, "I can envision a situation where the administration might say, 'Well, I know that person is only third on your list, but as long as this person is acceptable, why don't you make the offer to that person?' just because the person is a woman or a black." He went on, "To me, that is reverse discrimination . . . in this department, we'll hire the best person who's available, as opposed to hiring somebody who maybe is not as good, who is either a woman or a minority, or whatever, just to enforce affirmative action."

In similar vein, the chair of a department that had just terminated the appointment of an African-American man for lack of publications, when asked about the departmental climate for women and minorities, declared, "There's no difference here for women and minorities. It's impossible for everyone. It's sink or swim." The idea that some may have more "cultural capital" and learn to "swim" faster than others did not seem to be a consideration.

At some institutions, we spoke with fewer than five minority professors. In others we spoke with a very racially and ethnically diverse group, or with a core group of African Americans. At one institution, we interviewed Chicanos, Chicanas, Native Americans, and Asians. In another we interviewed a Chicana, a Central American, and two African Americans. Overall we interviewed 22 African Americans, 15 Latinos/as, 6 Asian Americans, and 2 Native Americans. In several instances, we will use the generic label "minority" to refer to a particular individual rather than his or her race (e.g., African American) or ethnicity (e.g., Chicano) in order to conceal the identity of the faculty member. We are fully aware that minorities do not constitute a monolithic group, and we use the generic "minority" only as a means of protecting the identity of participants. If the identity is not discernable, we shall identify individuals by race and/or ethnic background.

Our intent in this chapter is to touch on themes that figured prominently in the interviews of minority faculty such as the similarities and differences of minority faculty members' experiences in white academe; the strategies they employ to survive and succeed; and institutional and departmental practices that contribute to the affirmation and integration of "different" faculty members.

The Initiation of Minority Faculty

Interviews with minority faculty made it clear that the account with which we opened this chapter was not an anomaly. Like the Native-American woman, most minority faculty members described their interviews as a positive experience. They were impressed with the caliber of the faculty and students, and sensed that the institution would be a good place to begin or continue their academic careers. They were attracted to their institutions for different reasons: Some mentioned the teaching mission, or being more comfortable in a small institution, or wanting to work in an urban area, or the presence of like-minded colleagues. A Central-American professor said, "I valued what this college was trying to do in terms of its commitment to social issues—to issues of social justice and to issues of women and minorities . . . and that they were sensitive to my interest in working in Central America."

None of the minority faculty we interviewed said that they were made to feel uncomfortable or that they were token candidates. Nothing was said or done that caused them to be apprehensive about the institutional climate for minorities. Obviously institutions put their best efforts into wooing candidates. One institution demonstrated its seriousness about a candidate by scheduling private one-to-one meetings with the president and a trustee as part of the interview itinerary. He told us, "I met with the president and was very much taken and impressed by him. I also met students. And I had lunch with a trustee who chairs the sub-committee for academic affairs."

Needless to say, the VIP treatment that this professor received was quite exceptional. Nevertheless, large and small institutions, as well as wealthy and poor institutions, succeeded in presenting themselves in interviews as inviting and congenial places. An African-American woman, "doing a university-type interview" for the first time, was apprehensive about "underplaying" her qualifications. However, she was surprised and relieved to find "the people very welcoming and very inviting. I walked away feeling rather confident about the possibilities," she said. An Asian professor observed, "The faculty here had a nice rapport with each other and with me," whereas, "Some of the other places made me feel more on the spot during the interview, and so they seemed less warm." An African-American woman found that, "It was a very pleasant process, very conversational. The public lecture was a simulated classroom rather than a presentation to peers. I found that very comfortable. My sense is that was the most important part of the process." A Native American woman said,

> I had two days of interviews. I started out at nine in the morning and I taught a class, and then I had separate interviews with probably eight to ten people. There was a luncheon with a faculty group and I also had a meeting with the dean, and I ate dinner with the head of the department. I was impressed. It was a real comprehensive kind of interview. For instance, I had to teach a class, and that was interesting to me. The faculty were knowledgeable about me and interested in my employment.

Scheduling private one-on-one meetings and more informal gatherings with minority faculty proved to be very important in influencing how candidates judged institutions. An African-American male said, "One of the good things that happened was that I was introduced to other black faculty who were not part of the interview process, and that was very helpful. It was helpful because they talked about what it means to be a faculty person [at this institution] from a black perspective, and you know, they tell you things off the record, so you get the message. They'll give you the real deal, and on balance, they were very positive about this place."

A Chicana being considered for a joint appointment in a "straight" discipline-based department and Ethnic Studies[2] described the contrast between the two interviews. The department interview "was much more research and productivity oriented. People were much more interested in what I was going to teach and what my research agenda was." A little self-consciously she added,

> This is going to sound very stereotypical, but I have to say that to some extent my interviews with the staff and faculty in Ethnic Studies were much more personal. They were much more textured. We talked a lot about where we were from, how we had gotten to the positions we were in now, and that kind of thing. They wanted to know more about me and how I had become a professor in [Ethnic Studies].

In contrast, that "sort of personal connection" was not part of the interview in the discipline-based department, even though they were "very friendly and collegial."

The interview process can be far more intense and tiring for minority

---

[2] To protect the identify of faculty, we identify all ethnic focused programs and departments (e.g., Africana Studies, Puerto Rican Studies, Native American Studies, etc.) generically as Ethnic Studies.

candidates because they are often recruited for positions that are shared between a discipline and an ethnic studies program, or between a discipline and an ethnic studies research center, or, in the case of minority women, between a discipline and women's studies. A professor being considered by three different departments told us, "I actually got sick. There were a lot of interests for me to try to serve. I needed to please several different audiences. My schedule was very full. Every meal was an interview. There really wasn't a whole lot of down time, and I never saw a bit of the city." She ended by saying, "It was more intense than what I have heard from my friends and colleagues who interviewed only in this department."

First Impressions: The Campus Arrival

Some institutions managed to maintain the positive tone established during the interview by preparing for the newcomer's arrival on campus. The same Native-American woman who praised the interview process earlier in this chapter said, "I can't tell you how impressed I was by how well they took care of me from the moment I arrived." She went on,

> I was able to obtain one of the university houses. I arrived in the afternoon. One of the classes was just letting out, and most of the students just came over and moved my things out of the moving van into the house. It was very hot and the neighbors brought over some drinks. It was just a very, a very good welcome.

Two days later, she went to her office for the first time:

> When I got to my office my name was on the door, I already had name cards on my desk, and a whole array of office supplies on the desk that were ordered before I came. I have a beautiful office with a beautiful window. I was given a brand new big computer. I did not request or demand these things. My chair made it happen.

In seeing how much work and thought the chair had put into making her office ready, the Native-American newcomer said "it made me feel proud, positive, and pleased that I was being treated so well."

The Native-American woman's experience was not as rare as one might expect. In the same institution, an African-American woman said of her arrival, "It was quite nice, I actually thought it was a very smooth transition. The university has houses that they rent to the new faculty. It was nice to be able to come and not have to worry about where I was going to live, and that was all set up before I came. I felt very comfortable on campus. I immediately received a computer. My office was there, waiting and clean. I can't recall any surprises or disappointments initially."

In the case of minority faculty, particularly in institutions where there are few others like themselves, the actions of a department chair can dispel or exacerbate the discomfort of being the conspicuous Other. Take the case of an African-American woman who "missed the first faculty meeting because no one thought of giving me a key to the mail room, which I didn't even know existed." Most likely this was an oversight by a forgetful department chair or an overworked secretary. Even an honest and innocent mistake such as this can reinforce the outsider status of minority persons in predominantly white institutions.

Newcomers should not be expected to orient themselves by figuring out what questions to ask. We were surprised when a minority professor said, "My time is so taken up with getting the little things done that I have over-looked the department chair." We think it should be the other way around. It is the chair's responsibility to take care of the "little things" in order to keep new faculty members from being overwhelmed. The chair should also find time to meet with the new faculty rather than leaving it to chance encounters in the hallways.

"Things get done by people talking to each other," said an African-American woman, "but . . . the trick is knowing *what* and *who* to ask." Smaller institutions that function informally and on a more personal level have an even greater responsibility for orienting minority newcomers than larger institutions in which the newcomer can rely on the formal administrative structure and standard operating procedures. The chair or dean who tells new faculty, "If you have any questions, just ask," and leaves it at that, will be helpful only to those newcomers who know what questions to ask and who would not hesitate to call the dean or provost or department chair to schedule a meeting. We interviewed only a few newcomers who were secure and confident enough to ask questions or initiate relationships with senior professors.

Institutions that seek racial and ethnic minority group applicants have a responsibility to make sure that they are treated equitably. The chair and senior faculty should let the newcomer know that he or she is valued as a colleague. Thus when a dean knows that "a lot of the socialization is done at the department level" and is well aware that "some department chairs are better than others in taking faculty under their wings," it is disingenuous for him to overlook a chair's indifference because "another senior colleague will do what the chair should have done" or because "the junior faculty will initiate a meeting if they have questions."

Promotion and Tenure

Undoubtedly, the most critical quality for good leadership in terms of the retention of minority faculty is providing them with a thorough understanding of the requirements for tenure and promotion and the resources they need to fulfill these requirements. The following are some answers minority faculty gave when asked: "What do you have to do here in order to be promoted and obtain tenure?"

A Chicana said, "I wish someone would tell me what exactly I need to do. What we get told is that we need to publish in the highest quality journals. That the research needs to make a contribution to the discipline and needs to be recognized by other researchers." An African-American woman admitted, "I've been here for two years, and I am still trying to figure out exactly what's going on here and how I fit." Another said, "I'm female. I'm Native American. This faculty and this town and this university are very white. I would expect I would have to be a little better than average, than most. I would expect that I would have to be a little bit more clean than most. And by that I mean to not have conflicts with people. I would expect that I would need to be seen probably as a person who plays with the team." An African-American man said something similar: "I would say that the obvious criteria are committee work, teaching, and then research and writing. And then I would say, unofficially, things that would be important and taken into account would be getting along with people and not getting involved with a lot of the politicking."

The ambiguity of how quality is determined was also of concern for minorities. In a department that "graded" publications according to whether they appeared in "First Tier," "Second Tier," or "Third Tier" journals, with negative grades for articles that appear in a "glossy publication with a picture of the author," the criteria were still hard to decipher. A Chicana said, "It has never been laid out too clearly for me." "For example," she said:

> If you have one single-author article in a top journal that everybody cites and then a whole lot of secondary stuff, is that enough? Or if you have five or six pretty good articles in secondary or specialty journals, is that enough? Is that equivalent to having one really great article and a whole lot of book chapters? Do you have to have a book?

An African-American man with an excellent publications and grants record, who was about to be granted tenure and promoted to associate professor, told us, "There is the official handbook and then there is the little talk in the coffee area, hanging out with colleagues, which is another sort of educating process." Nevertheless, he pointed out, "There needs to be more systematic working with the new faculty person, about what to expect. . . ." He continued, "I'm the type of person who just will go out and have lunch and go drinking with anybody who'll tell me what's going on. But somebody who doesn't have that personality or isn't politically aware may be surprised. . . ." Ideally, "We should have an opportunity each year to talk about the tenure process. You know, how are you doing. . . ."

To be as self-initiating as the professor above requires self-assurance and a basic understanding of departmental politics. The direct manner of this professor and his assurance in dealing with senior faculty and members of the upper administration are not typical of the great majority of junior faculty members, minority or non-minority. For example, an African American whose contract was not renewed after four years said, "I don't know how to ask people for help, and they don't know or don't care to give it." The chair's failure to be a mentor had disastrous consequence for this professor. He said, "I'm damaged goods now. I wasn't that far behind. I was salvageable, and if they had sat down with me, we could have worked it out rather than proving they were right (not to renew his contract). My career is over even though I have two more years. I'm ruined."

In the previous chapter, we mentioned that the term "junior faculty" has connotations that reinforce the conditional status of those on the tenure-track. When status and power differences are made obvious, for example, through the division of labor (e.g., all the introductory courses are delegated to junior faculty and all the graduate seminars are taught by senior faculty), it should not be surprising if newcomers are cautious about their exchanges with senior faculty. For example, the African-American woman who told us, "I have had faculty not speak to me, ignore me," is less likely to seek information or advice from senior faculty than the Chicano who says "A lot of senior faculty take interest in my work and provide me with informal mentoring."

In institutions where minority faculty have a strong sense of community and solidarity, they assumed the responsibility for informing newcomers about the intricacies of tenure and promotion. Even the African-American man whose socialization fit the conventional model perfectly (e.g., he had developed collegial relations with senior faculty, had established a solid research agenda, had a better-than-average publishing record, and had won prestigious fellowships) remarked, "If it weren't for Ethnic Studies, I am not sure I would still be here." He explained that for him,

> Ethnic Studies provides an environment where there's sharing and networking. There is a web, and you can learn a lot of different things that you wouldn't

necessarily learn. You always feel comfortable approaching people there, and when you talk to people in Ethnic Studies, you know they are interested in you.

He pointed out, "There is an eagerness to share documents. 'This is my tenure file, this is what I did, let's get together, let me show you.'" When the time came for putting together his application for tenure, he said, "They showed me how to put the personal statement together. . . . One of my colleagues spent three hours with me, and we went through everything." He added, "In my department this kind of help would not be offered, I would have had to initiate it. You know what I mean?"

Similarly, a Chicana said, "I learned through Ethnic Studies [as opposed to Women's Studies] because women are not automatically aligned with each other, so my first support came not from other women but from Ethnic Studies, and they were all male. I learned all my survival strategies, all my techniques, from Ethnic Studies folk."

A national Chicana Studies organization also proved to be "a real training ground" for Latinas. A professor who benefitted from the organization's mentoring told us, "I came straight out of graduate school, and we were taught to be professors, not teachers, so I didn't learn how to teach. The associate professors [in Chicana Studies Organization] would say to us: 'Look, this is what we went through, formally and informally.' I was shown how to put together a class, how to handle problems in the classroom. They told us: 'You're a Latina and you're going to have white male students who've never seen a person like yourself in authority. This is how we deal with these type of things. . . . ' so it was really very helpful, very supportive."

An African-American woman who was the "only one" in her institution said, "What I've done is to set up a network that is not tied to my department. I figured out that I need a network to look at my work, make suggestions, and so forth. If I hadn't realized that, I would be wandering around aimlessly." Her network consists of an interdisciplinary women's writing group that meets once or twice a month. The only nonwhite member in the group, she described the importance of having such a network in light of her current situation: "I have an article right now that I'm ready to send out for publication and I know I can't go to the senior faculty and ask, 'Well what do you think about this article?' or 'I am thinking about this journal . . . do you have any suggestions?'" She added, "I don't think that I can go to the senior faculty and have them look at my mid-tenure self-appraisal and say, 'What do you think about this?' Because I don't think they are professionally alive and I don't trust what they would say." She also said, "I will probably go to my writing group and have them review my prospectus. That's the way I'm going to manage this mid-tenure review."

The suggestion to network is sound advice for virtually anyone. However, networking is of critical importance for individuals who differ from the norm, primarily because they may have no other alternative source of support. A white male faculty member in the sciences may feel comfortable with his colleagues to an extent that a minority faculty member often does not. Not only would we recommend that minority faculty network, but we also suggest that such networking needs to be encouraged and more formally structured.

Five minority women mentioned having learned about tenure and promotion serendipitously. A Chicana serving on a Women's Studies search committee said, "The woman we were interviewing asked the chair, 'What do you expect for tenure?' and the chair told her, 'You need a book, you need this many journal articles.' I just sat back and thought, 'At least she knows.' Nobody ever told me that." And a Latina who had a one-course release in order to participate in a weekly seminar on curricular change in Spanish said,

> El seminario es sobre "Diversity." Pero en realidad lo que mas se habla es de "tenure," los "pitfalls de tenure.

> The seminar is on diversity. But actually what we speak about mostly is tenure, the pitfalls of tenure.

> En el seminario aprendi muchas cosas que no sabia . . . los mecanismos de enviar cartas externas, los problemas que pueden ocurrir cuando el "dossier" sale . . . unos detalles muy tecnicos.

> In the seminar, I learned many things I did not know . . . the procedures for getting external letters of evaluation, the problems that can surface when the dossier leaves the department . . . and many other technical details about the tenure process.

An African-American woman who would be coming up for tenure in the following year said, "None of my colleagues have seen me teach . . . I don't know how they are going to evaluate me. . . . I have been reassured that it will be very pro-forma . . . but they did not give me any specific information as to what I need to do. . . . I spoke with the director of women's studies and asked her for more details . . . what people I should designate as readers, internally and externally, and that was very helpful."

Minority faculty in the social sciences whose research and publications fall under the general rubric of "ethnic/race/postcolonial" studies encounter obstacles that, as one professor put it, are symptomatic of "academic ethnocentrism." A Latino with a book published in Central America complained about the lack of "guidelines for evaluating books published in other countries and languages." "Third World presses," he pointed out, "do not enjoy the same luxuries as those in the U.S.—their books don't look handsome. . . . The quality of the paper and of the print makes them look less authoritative than a book published here." "Since senior faculty in evaluation committees rely on the North American academic canon as their frame of reference to make judgments about scholarship, '*se valora solamente lo que se publica aqui*' [only what is published in the U.S. is valued]." He went on to observe, "Books published in the Third World look flimsy; they are not sturdy like the books published in the U.S." Based on his own experience, this professor contended that if a book looks unattractive, is written in a language of "lesser status," and is published in a country that one associates with underdevelopment, poverty, and unpredictability, it is more susceptible to a biased review.

As noted when we discussed the interview process, the preponderance of split appointments among minorities, particularly in the humanities and social sciences, can lead to trouble in the evaluation process. A Chicana said, "The major problem, which is Major with a capital M, is that I was hired to teach Ethnic Studies, but Ethnic Studies is not a department, so my appointment is one hundred percent in [DISCIPLINE AREA], and it is a tug-of-war between how much time I give to each." She described tenure and promotion evaluations for faculty with split appointments as "contentious" because "Ethnic Studies is not regarded as a legitimate academic field." Consequently, she wondered, "If I publish in an Ethnic Studies journal and I don't have anything published in a straight [DISCIPLINE] journal, does that mean that I am below average? Or, if all my colleagues in the department serve on two committees, but I serve only on one because I also serve on two Ethnic Studies committees, does that mean that my service in the department is below average?" An African American expressed similar concerns: "The question is, who has the final say? Is it the department or Ethnic Studies? We have this document, and I am trying to interpret the fine print, but it's never been pushed as to who has the power to make the final determination."

Few minority faculty members had been assigned mentors even at those institutions that claimed to have a formal mentoring system for new faculty. Thus a professor might be told in a written evaluation to "solidify your research agenda" without senior faculty offering their assistance. An African-American woman in her second year, struggling to develop a plan of work, said, "I've spent a lot of time trying to figure out how to perceive my scholarship. You know, where I should go now. I've done this dissertation; what's my next step as a scholar and as a teacher?"

Institutions with faculty development programs sent out announcements of their services, but the minority and non-minority faculty who took advantage of such services were few. An African American who was among those few said, "I was here a year before I knew they had a mentoring program." Once he found out about the program, he said:

> I chose a mentor and it's been a very positive relationship. It's very important as far as I am concerned, in terms of understanding this particular system and setting my priorities so that by the time the tenure clock rolls around, I will be ready.

He described how he benefitted from this relationship:

> He gives me helpful suggestions on how to get things accomplished, what things to look out for . . . that I should keep an eye out for the internal grants and when proposals are due. He also has told me to keep an eye out for the sorts of programs that tend to be funded and what kinds of things are not likely to get funded . . . essentially how to target proposals to catch the eye of individuals that are making the decisions about internal grants.

Teaching-oriented institutions had mentoring programs to strengthen teaching, to diversify the curriculum, and to introduce faculty to alternative teaching methods. A Latina said, "I was paired with a female instructor who had been here for several years, and we team-taught . . . so I learned a lot from her because she was mentoring me along and working with me." Another institution had a "Partners in Learning" program that paired faculty to observe each other and provide feedback. An African-American woman who volunteered as a participant said, "I decided to take advantage of it because I enjoy learning about teaching methods, and since it is not part of the evaluation process, there was not any sense of threat. It's a wonderful idea. My partner and I talked freely about what we observed in each other's class and about the responses of students to different methods."

The minority faculty who were most productive according to conventional standards for research and scholarship had their own research agendas as well as previous experience in publishing, either as graduate students or from having worked in research-related organizations prior to joining the faculty. These professors directed their energies toward research and writing and looked for ways to reduce their teaching responsibilities. For example, a generous fellowship from a private foundation made it possible for an African-American professor to be released from all teaching responsibilities and spend two years conducting research and writing. A Chicano was able to rearrange his schedule not to teach for one semester in order to finish a book.

In other words, minority faculty who were productive according to traditional measures of scholarship had internalized the norms of the research university culture: They arranged their schedules in order to write; they spent time conducting research; they were selective about their involvement in campus activities; they did not allow their teaching responsibilities to overwhelm them; they applied for grants; they solicited comments on their written work. Minority professors whose work habits conformed to this profile were more likely to have entered graduate school immediately after earning their baccalaureate degrees. Their doctorates were from nationally recognized universities, including Harvard, the University of Chicago, the University of Texas at Austin, the University of California at Berkeley, and the Union Theological Seminary.

The Burdens of Cultural Taxation

While lack of mentors, ambiguous information, and limited experience thwarted research productivity among minority faculty, these circumstances are not unique to this group. White faculty also experience feelings of vulnerability and uncertainty on the tenure track. The major element of academic life that works uniquely against minority faculty is the burden of "cultural taxation." According to Padilla,

> "Cultural taxation" is the obligation to show good citizenship toward the institution by serving its needs for ethnic representation on committees, or to demonstrate knowledge and commitment to a cultural group, which may even bring accolades to the institution but which is not usually rewarded by the institution on whose behalf the service was performed. (1994, p 26)

Minority faculty are involved in a variety of activities that typify cultural taxation. An assistant professor said, "My life is really overwhelmingly busy in terms of service. Service counts for only twenty percent of the evaluation, and I do three to four times as much as any [other] faculty person." He continued,

> Because I am Latino, I get a fairly substantial trickle of minority students who come here, not necessarily to be advised in the traditional, more formal sort of way, but just to come by to talk and explore their problems, to tell me that they can't handle this institution anymore because it is so white. Or to let me know that a situation at home is intolerable . . . so I have that kind of double role to

play in terms of academic but also more of a personal advisor role, and that takes up a lot of my time.

At the end he remarked, "The institution does not recognize that minority faculty have an extra load by being minorities. . . . I enjoy doing it, but it needs to be rewarded."

A research university addressed the problem of cultural taxation in the promotion guidelines, stating that:

> When evaluating women and minority academic professionals, continuing status and promotion committees should be watchful for the "hidden workload" of especially burdensome advising responsibilities and committee work. Women and minority professionals who work with students often attract large numbers of advisees who look to their advisors as mentors and role models. Furthermore, women and minority professionals are commonly assigned a disproportionately heavy load of committee work as an outgrowth of the need for diverse committee composition. Given these circumstances, it is especially important that the extent of advising, committee responsibilities, and related tasks be fully documented for women and minority professionals, and that such activities be given their due weight in continuing status and promotion deliberations.

An African-American woman said she was expected to "provide a role model for African American students and be an ad hoc advisor . . . to be a Black authority and in a vague, very general way to provide diversity to the campus." Minority faculty fulfill the expectation—apparent even though not directly articulated—of "providing diversity" in several ways. For example, a woman said, "I was asked to be present at a number of interviews, partly because I was a junior minority woman, and they didn't want those interviews to have only senior white men, especially because they are looking for minority candidates." An African-American woman said, "I am asked to speak a lot, to participate in things, and I think it's because they need an African American . . . so that gets a little bit tiring but I have not said 'no' too much. People will call me to sit on ad hoc committees," and, with a knowing laugh, she added, "They call me more than occasionally." A Chicana said, "They expect me to be an expert on Latinos. . . . They will say things like, 'Well, you are Mexican, so answer me this question.'" A Native-American woman said, "I get sick to death of being the novelty, of people speaking to me just because I'm Indian . . . I don't care for that. I am a person." An African American said, "I was asked to go on trips to recruit minority graduate students. . . . It was personally gratifying but beyond the call of duty, and I wonder about tenure."

A less-talked-about form of cultural taxation has to do with the commodification of race or ethnicity to make an institution look good. An administrator said, "We got one," in reference to an African American. "He has social skills that most other people don't . . . he is very charismatic and very photogenic . . . every time there is an activity, it's so nice to have him out there in front . . . and he gets asked all the time. . . . He loves that kind of stuff." Even so, there is concern that despite his being "enormously popular with students" and "actively involved in service," this assistant professor needs to give more attention to research and scholarship and concentrate on publications. His outgoing personality and good looks make him an ideal symbol of diversity, but obviously neither "charisma" nor "photogenicity" are acceptable substitutes for published research, not even if the individual is a superb teacher and an outstanding citizen of the department and college.

Similarly, an African-American woman in an institution with only a few African Americans on the faculty said, "I am often taken into places that feel a little bit uncomfortable. . . . Next month I will moderate a university-wide panel that is part of a major lecture series . . . and I have not done that kind of thing before. . . . Sometimes I wonder what people expect of me." On one hand, it is flattering for a new faculty member to be asked to represent the university in public forums. On the other hand, minorities are sometimes overwhelmed by the burden of the institution's shortage of minority representation, and many end up forfeiting their academic careers. This individual, for example, will be highly visible in the institution, but she is unlikely to receive the mentoring she is seeking:

> I've spent a lot of time trying to figure out how to proceed with my scholarship. You know, where should I go now? I've done this dissertation, what's my next step, as a scholar and as a teacher. I have so many little projects out there, and people are going to want to hear where these projects are going, and I realize that I need direction . . . I need someone to help me figure that out.

Minority faculty may also be more susceptible to taking on extra service burdens because it provides a means of making connections and finding out what is going on. For example, we asked an African-American woman, "What would happen if you said no the next time you are asked to participate in a committee?" "You know what would happen," she said, "I'd feel like I'd be missing something . . . so it's not all the college's fault, it's me, too." Perhaps she is correct in thinking that the college is not entirely to blame. However, if information were disseminated freely and there were an ethos of inclusiveness, she might be less concerned about "missing something."

Minority Existences in White Academia: Individual Survival and Institutional Transformation

Minority faculty often find themselves in departments where they are the token "Other" or in institutions where they are one of a small group of "Others." In predominately white institutions, they continually confront manifestations of institutionalized ethnocentrism and racism. A Japanese man who had no friends at the institution said, "It has been the loneliest year of my life." As the token African American or Latino in departmental and university committees, minority faculty members are often placed in the uncomfortable position of acting as advocates for minority interests because no one else will do it. Often they are the only outspoken supporters of affirmative action. "Every committee I serve on, I'm the only minority," said an African American, and "usually I am the one to raise issues about minorities." Being the sole defender of affirmative action frequently places a minority in conflict with their senior colleagues. An African American serving on a search committee said, "We were discussing announcements for faculty openings and I said we should make sure we have emphasis on people of color, and they said, 'Oh, we'll tag on that standard thing.' They just didn't get my message. You sometimes get dismissed, you know, around issues like that." Speaking out for affirmative action is also difficult in the presence of senior faculty and administrators who, in the guise of excellence, are opposed to doing more than what is legally required to be in compliance with affirmative action guidelines. Oppositional stances between minority and majority colleagues on policies and practices intended to correct discriminatory hiring practices underscore the power and status differences that define them as outsiders and insiders, respectively. As long as theirs are the only voices raised on behalf of minorities, minority faculty will be reminded of their "outsider" status. Even worse, the African-American or Latino professor whose efforts to recruit minorities are interpreted as "favoritism," "quota filling," "preferential hiring" or the "lowering of academic standards" is bound to wonder whether his colleagues view him as a "target-of-opportunity" hire.

In a conversation with two African-American professors about the virtual absence of minority faculty in their respective institutions and how it affects them personally, one said, "Yeah, it's not in their [white senior faculty] consciousness." And the other said, "I had to set my chair straight, to realize that when you hire an African-American woman, you just haven't hired a new faculty member. . . . It means that the environment has changed, and that I may need to have other African-American women to talk with, to visit with. . . ."

The comments of a young professor who was the sole African American at an institution for the first three years of his appointment indicate the importance of building a core group of minority faculty:

> I always felt that I could be close to the other faculty, especially here in my department, I will admit that. But in terms of other faculty of color, I think that there may be experiences that are unique to us, you know, our experiences of going through a graduate program as the only black and our experiences dealing with the world at large.

> 'Yes, you have a Ph.D. Yes, you know you have an education, you have gotten the highest degree that you can attain, and YES, WE'RE STILL TREATED LIKE NOBODIES.' I don't think a white instructor could feel what it is like. This is something that I can talk about with other black faculty.

In a matter of two years, this professor witnessed the number of African-American faculty at his institution grow from one to seven. Speaking about the changed composition of the faculty, he observed, "Now I have counterparts that I can count on as comrades." "It really is a sort of social and emotional support network . . . which is different than the academic support network, which I always felt here . . . I always felt there were people I could talk to about academic issues, what we expect from students, and things like that. . . . It's a little bit more difficult to discuss other things and have them understand what it's like for a black man in this institution and in this area of the country." With his black colleagues, he said,

> We can talk about the experience of walking down the street and having someone clutch their purse . . . it is not an experience I can talk about with someone who's in their fifties, who is white, who is maybe of an Irish background, and who would be able to understand it. You know, it is a little difficult to explain how frustrated I am when I'm jogging and I see people flinch away from me, when that should not be. You can get [white] people who will say, 'Yeah, I understand.' But that's not really understanding. When you have lived through it, I mean, the moment it comes out of your mouth, another black person goes: 'Yeah, yeah, yeah, I know exactly what you're talking about.'

Few institutions have the capacity, the strategy, policies, or boldness to hire with the specific intent of creating a core group of African-American or Latino or Asian or Native-American faculty. The benefits to the individual minority of having others with a shared social and cultural experience are obvious from the candid comments of the African-American male who started out being the first black faculty member hired and now is one of several minority faculty. Obviously, having "comrades," as he put it, increases the likelihood that he will wish to remain at the institution. It also makes the institution more attractive for other minority scholars.

At another small liberal arts college the few African-American faculty members were reluctant to get together as a group on campus. They wished to avoid the appearance of being separatists. One African American put it this way: "All of the black folks on campus get together a couple of times a semester . . . but strangely, we get together off-campus, as if we're afraid. . . . I tell them: 'Let's go to the campus center and be seen,' . . . you know, there's power in that."

A premise of this book is that new faculty are socialized into the cultures of their departments and that their entry also changes the existing cultures. As has been shown, one of the ways in which minority faculty attempt to change the culture of the academy is by raising consciousness about the importance of hiring minority candidates. However, attempting to change the culture of departments and institutions can be an alienating experience. The strain a minority person goes through to make him- or herself fit into academic cultures that they are also struggling to make less alienating for others can be exhausting and demoralizing, as the observations of an African-American woman revealed:

> I spent last year being very angry, and this year I have put my efforts in trying to understand. The first understanding I have arrived at is that I don't think these guys understand that we can't operate the way they did fifteen years ago. So, it does me no good to be angry. I don't think they are used to working with an assertive woman, and I don't think they are used to working with an African-American woman. So, I have two choices: I can stay angry, or I can back off, observe more, and try to be more communicative. If I stay angry, I will distance myself, which is very easy to do. You know, I am really trying to minimize the amount of energy that I put into being angry and upset about things that smack against my sense of fairness.

Minority hiring is often prompted by pressure from constituencies, internal and external to the institution, to close the racial gap in the professoriat. In all the institutions we visited, minorities were severely underrepresented. In some cases, the recruitment of minority faculty was specifically linked to a newly articulated multicultural mission or a renewed commitment to democratic aims. For example, the sevenfold increase in the number of African-American faculty at one institution was integral to a mission explicitly tied to the racial, ethnic, and class backgrounds of a predominantly inner-city student body. Minority faculty were recruited to participate in the transformation of the institution. An African-American professor said, "We are probably one of the few colleges that has a clear mission statement that indicates what we are trying to do, and as long as we continue to do that, I will be interested in staying here." This professor dedicated part of his time to the "African American Male Student Support Program," which matches African-American male students with a faculty mentor for the duration of their undergraduate education. As a mentor, he spends time with young black males, hanging out in the dormitory, eating in the cafeteria, and going to student activities. This professor's involvement is valued and recognized as service that embodies and sustains the institution's mission.

In contrast, at an institution where "diversity" and "multiculturalism" in the curriculum were being strongly promoted along with an educational philosophy based on an ethic of compassionate justice for the poor, the faculty evaluation system was not aligned with the institutional mission. Minority faculty who had been attracted to the institution by its "social justice" mission found, as one professor put it, that "we are not held accountable to [the mission] in what we teach, what we write on, or the service we provide." Another professor said, "The service that I provide to Hispanic students is not recognized by the department." An African American said, "The mission is a smoke screen . . . it makes the institution look good. . . . I am certain that the faculty could not state it. . . . "

We have hardly mentioned whether minority faculty spoke about having experienced racism. The great majority of minority faculty did not allude to acts of overt racism. However, this does not necessarily mean that they had not experienced racism. For example, when we asked, "What is it like to be an African-American woman on this campus?" one of our interviewees said,

> I am still trying to figure that one out. I never know how people are reacting to me. Like last night, several of my colleagues were at the lecture, and actually, the only two people who said something to me were from different departments. And so I didn't get any feedback, and I wondered, Well, now, why is this? Was I terrible, or did I do something, did I make a faux pas that I wasn't aware of? It's really difficult, not getting the feedback, and not knowing why I'm not getting the feedback.

Once again she repeated, "I don't know how people are reacting to me, I don't know if I don't get feedback because I am African American, or because I am junior faculty." She continued,

> I speak to people, I say, 'Good morning.' And some people ignore that . . . maybe it is this region of the country. I've even been approaching faculty and making eye contact, and they would turn away . . . so I don't know if it's the culture of the city, the college, or my being African American.

One explanation of why so little was said about racism may be that it is very difficult to talk about institutionalized forms of racism without sounding overly sensitive or appearing unwilling to assume personal responsibility for individual shortcomings. It is possible that minorities in general and African Americans more specifically are under a great deal of social pressure not to blame their situations on racism, e.g., not getting information, being left out of informal networks, being ignored, or being expected to speak for their entire race or ethnic group, etc.[3] bell hooks (1989) is particularly helpful in making us see that even when racism is not named, it is still experienced by black faculty, particularly in settings that purport to be free of prejudice and discrimination. She says,

> While it is true that the nature of racist oppression and exploitation has changed as slavery had ended and the apartheid structure of Jim Crow has legally changed, white supremacy continues to shape perspectives on reality and to inform the social status of black people and all people of color. Nowhere is this more evident than in university settings. And often it is the liberal folks in those settings who are unwilling to acknowledge this truth. (p 114)

Comments made by minority faculty reveal the omnipresence of racism in predominantly white settings:

> African-American woman: "I still feel myself a stranger. That is, I am comfortable [but] not at home";

> African man: "Last year at this time I thought 'I am getting out of here,' . . . it seemed like they did not trust me . . .";

> Native-American woman: "Soon after I started, I heard that the Head had boasted about getting a minority on the cheap."

None of these individuals described these actions as being specifically racist, even though they might easily have done so. Instead, they described these as normal experiences that should be expected in a white setting. It is this matter-of-fact approach that makes it so easy for white colleagues and decision makers to ignore the myriad ways in which racism is expressed and maintained. It seems that minorities are the only ones who are able to recognize racism and its effects on the everyday life of a minority junior professor in an all-white department. Our point is that white academic leaders need to

---

[3] We are indebted to Mr. Elton Crim, a doctoral student in Penn State's Higher Education Program, for having offered this interpretation.

learn to recognize the more common and nuanced forms of racism that persist in the academy.

Finally, we recognize that just as women's socialization experiences are different from men's, there will also be differences in the way women and men of color experience socialization. In this chapter we have not differentiated between the experiences of male and female faculty of color, because our data are too limited to make such comparisons. Most minority faculty we interviewed in a given department were the only minority junior person, and even though in a given institution we might have interviewed minority women and men, because of departmental differences as well as racial/ethnic background differences, it is very difficult to make such comparisons. To compensate for this limitation, we have identified throughout the text the sex of individual faculty so as not to leave the reader wondering whether "such and such experience" is more typical of, say, an African-American man or woman, or a Chicana or Chicano.

We now turn to a discussion of the data provided in the preceding three chapters and offer recommendations on how institutions might transform socialization processes.

CHAPTER 6

Rethinking Promotion and Tenure

> The only people who count are those who launch out on
> to unknown seas. One doesn't discover new lands without
> consenting to lose sight of the shore for a very long time.
> —André Gide, *The Counterfeiters*

Throughout this book, we have contended that the promotion and tenure
system as it exists in the late twentieth century is in need of dramatic overhaul. However, "dramatic overhaul" can be interpreted in any number of
ways. Some would recommend that tenure be abolished, while others might
argue that it would be sufficient to modify parts of the current system. In this
chapter, we shall offer suggestions for both interpretations.

Like Gide, we believe that the future will offer new intellectual territory
to discover even as this century did. Who could have conceived at the time
of the Ross case at Stanford, or even during the advent of federal funding for
research after World War II, that colleges and universities would be structured and staffed as they are now, or that student bodies would encompass
such wide diversity? May we not reasonably expect as much, if not even
more, change during the next century? Accordingly, we must "lose sight" of
the current shore in order to seek new academic horizons. But one does not
"launch out on to unknown seas" in vessels that are not seaworthy. Consequently, we need to reform and improve the current system of promotion and
tenure as we develop new organizational structures.

The Academic World as It Is

Reviewing the Data

We pointed out that individuals new to an institution undergo two forms of
socialization: anticipatory and organizational. We discussed anticipatory socialization from the perspective of job interviews and the period between
hiring and arrival on campus; organizational socialization involves an individual's initial experiences, his or her work life, mentoring, and the process
of promotion and tenure.

In addition to information about the constraints of the job market and the kind of work an individual desired, three points stand out with regard to anticipatory socialization. First, the job interview is usually an intense "blur" for most candidates, regardless of institutional type. Individuals go through a round robin of interviews, give a presentation to the faculty, and may have a formal meeting about the requirements of the job with a dean or departmental chair. Second, the contract that an individual signs and the work responsibilities delineated are highly individualized and may depend to a considerable extent on the knowledge and negotiation skills of the candidate. Third, formal and informal orientations were generally not provided. Although there may have been a meeting for new faculty prior to the start of the school year, most individuals saw these as bureaucratic and perfunctory. Similarly, some campuses expected individuals such as a departmental chair or an informal committee to provide initial advice and support; most had no arrangements of this nature. In general, individuals had to rely on their own intuition, or the kindness of departmental secretaries, other junior faculty, or graduate students to obtain basic information.

Once new faculty members arrived on campus and entered the second stage of socialization, they were not surprised to find a similar tenor to that of stage one. Mentoring was a haphazard process for most. Formal relationships were usually not initiated, and if they were, they often did not develop satisfactorily. A minority of interviewees said they did not want a mentor, but the vast majority did. Few individuals could articulate a clear idea of what they wanted, but they knew what they had was insufficient. Informal mentoring resulted from the desire for collegial relationships with senior faculty members, and again, discussions with the vast majority of interviewees revealed the absence of such interactions.

Throughout the interviews, it became apparent that more than one individual needed to act as a mentor for new faculty. An assistant professor has multiple needs—e.g., publishing, teaching, navigating the political terrain of the institution, and the like—and one person may lack the expertise, time, or inclination to provide support in all areas. Additionally, we pointed out that mentoring requires senior faculty to serve as examples of how to behave within the organization, as guides for navigating the academic waters, and as historians for interpreting institutional context.

Regardless of institutional type and discipline, junior faculty found themselves working virtually all the time. Weekends, summers, and holidays were occupied with preparing lesson plans, writing proposals, conducting research, or writing up the results of their research for professional journals. One of the most confusing aspects of their professional lives was that the tenure-track faculty were never sure how much they were expected to work.

Most individuals at large institutions or in departments that did not emphasize research felt that teaching was undervalued and they were not given incentives either to excel in the classroom or to improve their teaching. Smaller private institutions focused more on teaching than on research, but the criteria for what defined good teaching were as ambiguous as they were at large public universities. Student evaluations were the primary means for determining the quality of teaching, and in some institutions senior faculty evaluations were also used.

Research was important, but how it was defined was quite ambiguous. In fields such as engineering, most faculty saw proposal writing and the attainment of grants as part of the research process. In other fields, research counted only if the results were published in a refereed journal, and in still other areas, books counted more than articles. It was not surprising that the sciences attached more importance to multi-authored articles than a field such as education did, but seemed strange that individuals in the same department had different ideas about what was important. Recall the example of a dean saying that junior faculty should not publish outside of their respective disciplines, and the assistant professor saying that he anticipated no problem in being given credit for publications he had in journals that were essentially unrelated to his area.

Finally, with regard to the third aspect of faculty work, while service was not formally rewarded, it was often considered symbolically important. Individuals served on committees at various levels; as was the case with other aspects of their careers, they were never sure how much committee work was sufficient. Some new faculty members wanted to serve on committees, but were never asked to do so. Others estimated that they spent more than ten hours a week on committee assignments.

Every probationary faculty member hoped that all of his or her work brought the goal of promotion and tenure nearer. However, as noted previously, no one seemed to know exactly what was expected. Even the process itself was a mystery to most candidates. Information, if it may be called that, on the time frame, who was involved, and how dossiers were compiled was most often vague, if not downright contradictory. For example, individuals were told by a departmental chair to develop a dossier one way, only to be informed later by personnel in the dean's office that they must use another format. Who was qualified to provide an outside evaluation of a candidate was often problematic, and the systematic assessment of teaching was usually nonexistent except in the form of student evaluations.

We pointed out that individuals often felt emotionally and intellectually exhausted by the time tenure was conferred. We also noted that while initiates are socialized according to the present system, it is questionable whether the process succeeds in doing what is desirable from an institutional standpoint. We asked what the consequences were for an organization that social-izes individuals to the norms described throughout this text: Good teaching is not particularly valued, and service is often seen as a waste of time. Re-search is pursued not because of any intrinsic interest, but in order to attain job security. Collegial relationships are sporadic at best and intellectual con-versation appears to be on the verge of extinction.

An Organizational Framework for Excellence

The basic themes and dilemmas that emerged in this study are remarkably consistent with the findings of faculty socialization studies conducted by several other scholars (e.g., Boice 1992; Bronstein, Rothblum and Solomon 1993; Austin 1990; Sorcinelli 1992). Our intent in quoting directly the men and women who shared their experiences with us has been to depict life on the tenure track as honestly as possible and to illuminate its pitfalls. We turn now to a discussion of how the process might be improved so that individ-uals are socialized in a different manner, and in turn, develop a different sense of what it means to be a member of an academic community. If by generalization it is taken to mean a lock-step process in which every individ-ual at every institution is expected to act in a similar manner, then what we offer here will be seen as mistaken if not foolish. The interviews reveal that institutional context necessitates different interpretations, and even within the same institution individuals will have different ideas about what they need or what should be done to improve practice. Our suggestions, then, are strategic rather than "rules for socialization."

At the same time, we work from quite different assumptions than the conservative and liberal-humanist views outlined in chapter 1. We do not share the conservative view that contends the problem lies with individuals, nor do we accept the liberal-humanist view that assumes a consensual model of the academy. Critical postmodernism seeks to understand how an aca-demic community in which individual differences are honored might be con-structed. A consensual or collegial model of the organization is rejected in favor of a more protean interpretation of the culture of the institution. In-stead of thinking of socialization as a means to indoctrinate initiates into the mores of the culture, we regard it as a way to discover organizational beliefs and symbols, and to think about how such beliefs might change as individ-uals and contexts change.

From the interviews, we discovered individuals who work hard and try to meet often unclear and ambiguous goals. We also heard from faculty who differ from the norm because of their individual identities as women or peo-ple of color. Thus, we have developed a schema utilizing West's notion, as discussed in the first chapter; the intellectual perspective develops and enhances an academic community that honors difference and assumes individuals are not the problem. The processes and structure are the issue. Strategies, then, offer directions that academic leaders might call upon in their own institutions in order to refine and restructure the promotion and tenure processes.

Strategies for Anticipatory Socialization

Job announcements and job interviews give candidates an indication of the kind of environment in which they will find themselves if they are hired. If an institution's participants say that teaching is emphasized, it seems reasonable to expect some statement about teaching from the candidate in the job application. When the interview takes place, the individual should be asked to teach a class or at least speak with students.

Participants in an organization that honors difference will recognize that the job interview is a two-way process through which the interviewee also learns something about the college or university. A dean or senior faculty member who believes that she does not have the time to talk to a candidate might rethink her priorities. Similarly, an interview that does not give a candidate some sense of the local community and schools may not meet the individual's needs.

Candidates should be given the opportunity to ask questions and find out the requirements of the job. Similarly, as far as possible, the bargaining process that now exists in academe should be laid to rest. Conversely, candidates should be made aware what is reasonable to expect. The point is that when an unexperienced applicant accepts a faculty position and the dean does not provide adequate office space or support simply because the individual did not request it, two consequences are likely to occur. On one hand, the newcomer may arrive at the institution with a negative attitude: "If this is the way they are treating me from the start, what am I to expect?" On the other hand, the individual may interpret this as an implicit message that an academic community does not exist, and instead there is a climate, a hyperindividualism in which everyone must fight for his or her own resources. Socialization from this perspective is antithetical to the development of a community of difference.

The search committee should reconsider a number of actions that may occur during a candidate's interview. To be sure, sexist comments such as those reported in chapter 3 are easy to condemn; however, measures should also be taken to make the gamut that the candidate is required to run less arduous. In chapter 2 we outlined the dimensions of faculty socialization; a committee would be remiss if its members did not consider the kinds of initial experiences they want the candidate to have during his or her first days on campus. In the case of women and faculty of color, a private meeting with other women or faculty of color should be part of the interview process. As we showed in chapter 4, an all-male search committee can convey a negative message about the status of women in the department. Not having women or other faculty of color in the department does not exempt search committees from arranging opportunities for minority candidates to find out what it is like to be a woman or an African American or Chicano or Native American in a particular institution. Search committees should seek the opinions of Women's and Ethnic Studies faculty on ways to make the interview a positive experience and to show the campus as a good place for minority faculty.

Similarly, the period between hiring a new faculty member and his or her arrival on campus also needs more attention. One logical issue is deciding who will be responsible for working with the individual during the initial months. The search committee may have been adjourned, thinking their task is completed; the departmental chair may not feel that he or she should yet be involved, and the dean will be too busy. Again, our point is not to make a simplistic rule—"in all cases the department chair must be responsible"—but to encourage the organization's participants to think about who will help the recruit prior to his or her arrival on campus. A small liberal arts college developed a "survival guide" for new faculty, containing the kind of everyday information that can overwhelm a newcomer to a city or town, such as the location of banks, supermarkets, schools for children, daycare facilities, health clubs, special interest groups (e.g., the gay men's network), bookstores, coffee houses, gourmet stores, restaurants, travel agencies, etc.

As we proposed with mentoring, perhaps the optimal response is to have two individuals work with formal and informal tasks. Assistance with formal tasks, such as paperwork that must be completed or the creation of a dossier, should probably be provided by a unit head. Again, if such tasks are not done, or if they are done haphazardly, the message to the recruit is that such tasks—and the individual—are not very important. An individual should not arrive on campus to find that no one has considered what office he or she will have, or that a computer that was promised has not been ordered. Such oversights are thoughtless and reflect badly on the institution. Further, institutional actors need to know how to prevent "chilly climates." Recommended works dealing with women's issues include Bernice Sandler's "The Campus Climate Revisited: Chilly for Women Faculty, Administrators, and Graduate Students" (1986), Sarah Nieves-Squires' "Hispanic Women: Making their Presence on Campus Less Tenuous" (1993), and Yolanda Moses' "Black Women in Academe: Issues and Strategies" (1989).

Newcomers—particularly first-time faculty—usually have innumerable questions. We ought to be sensitive enough to arrange informal get-togethers so that questions can be answered in a comfortable atmosphere. For example, a new faculty member may not wish to ask what might be percieved as "dumb questions" of a department chair, and another may prefer to direct a personal question only to his or her immediate superior. Both avenues should be open to the individual, and it is incumbent on the organization's participants to see that they are.

We cannot emphasize enough that first impressions are indelible. If a department chair creates a casual atmosphere in which an individual feels that questions are welcome, then further down the tenure road one would expect the organizational climate to remain the same. A dean certainly should not micro manage the everyday affairs of a department within his or her jurisdiction, but it is inadvisable for the dean to refrain from any involvement whatsoever. Is it asking too much to expect a dean to make one phone call to a newly hired faculty member in the course of a summer, merely to say that he or she looks forward to an individual's arrival on campus? Such a phone call conveys a message of inclusion. It also lets the dean know whether the recruit's questions are being answered by others in the department or unit.

Strategies for Organizational Socialization

Mentoring

Someone should be designated as a formal mentor to provide structured, systematic feedback to an individual on an ongoing basis. Far too often, institutions opt for legal protection instead of honest dialogue. That is to say, legalistic letters to an untenured faculty member in trouble may get the institution off the hook, but it does little or nothing to promote the individual's professional development.

In most instances, one formal mentor will be the departmental chair. The chair should be responsible for making it clear to the individual on what basis he or she will be evaluated, aspects of his or her performance that need to be improved, and resources that are available to facilitate such improvement. The chair also can arrange mentoring relationships with other individuals at the institution.

We have also mentioned that an assistant professor may benefit from formal mentoring relationships in other domains. Research is usually generated by interest, but senior faculty should be encouraged to take more than a passing interest in the professional development of their junior colleagues. We heard, for example, from junior faculty who sought advice about where to submit proposals to fund their research. Senior faculty may have been willing or available to provide advice on this, but they did not consider it their responsibility to do so. We are suggesting that it is the responsibility of senior faculty and that they must be socialized to assume the role of mentor.

Further, when a senior faculty member becomes a mentor, it should not imply that he or she is always more knowledgeable on all matters. In research and teaching, everyone should strive for continual improvement. When discussions focus on both parties' intellectual engagement with a task, a more collegial environment is established, rather than one in which junior faculty are made to feel that they have nothing to offer and everything to learn.

Mentoring with regard to teaching is one area that needs more attention on college campuses. The standards that an institution uses to decide whether a candidate is a good teacher appear superficial and arbitrary. The assumption that a single item on an assessment by undergraduate students is sufficient to measure a faculty member's performance implies a low regard for teaching. Similarly, to have one senior professor observe an untenured colleague's class one semester and another professor do so at another time, with neither of them using standardized criteria for evaluation, is little short of absurd. Either such evaluations are trivial, or they should reflect consistently what the college defines as superior teaching. We find the comment that "you know good teaching when you see it" insufficient. If the evaluations are trivial then the institution should not waste faculty members' time with them; if they are important, then more thought should be given to their procedure and content.

Care should be taken not to penalize faculty for experimenting with teaching approaches intended to involve students more actively, such as feminist and critical pedagogies.

We are suggesting that individuals should think of the evaluation of teaching more as a *process* than as an *outcome*. Many of our informants remarked that senior faculty evaluations were little more than pro-forma exercises performed to satisfy bureaucratic requirements. Not only the department, but also the college and the institution would be better served by careful deliberation about the format for evaluation. If letters need to be placed in a faculty member's file, that is one step, but not the only one, toward the evaluation and improvement of teaching. Candidates deserve the opportunity to meet with their mentors regularly, and an institution that values distinguished teaching would implement a process whereby discussions about teaching are part of daily life in the organization, rather than formulaic rituals that are held in order to evaluate an individual faculty member.

Informal mentoring can occur at various levels and on virtually any occasion. An invitation to lunch suggests inclusion, whereas a separate table reserved for senior faculty only indicates the opposite. Social gatherings such as a holiday party or a school reception are made much easier if someone who "knows the ropes" offers to accompany someone who has recently arrived. In chapter 3, we reported that a certain departmental chair escorted his junior faculty to coffees at the college in order to make them feel more welcome. We are suggesting that such actions should be cultural norms rather than exceptions. A dean who only knows the names of the senior faculty makes it clear that he regards the untenured as unimportant. Conversely, a departmental chair who regularly has lunch with junior and senior faculty members primarily to stimulate communication will likely establish an atmosphere of openness, accessibility, and communication.

In chapters 4 and 5, we provided numerous examples of women and minority faculty being excluded from informal mentoring. Informal mentoring is likely to occur naturally among socially similar faculty. Therefore, it is important for senior faculty and academic administrators to be more deliberate about including "all" junior faculty in departmental insider circles that will facilitate publishing, conference presentations, and a more nuanced understanding of the professorial role. Interviews with women and faculty of color revealed that informal mentoring for these individuals was most likely to come from women's groups or other ethnic faculty. Institutions should provide resources to make such support groups possible and to reward senior women and minority faculty members who take on these mentoring responsibilities.

Dimensional Interactions

In chapter 2, we discussed the dimensions of faculty socialization. We return to them here to offer brief suggestions as to how an organization's participants might think of these dimensions and develop strategies for excellence.

Collective-Individual (group or individually oriented)

- Think of orientation as a dialogistic process rather than a session at which information is conveyed.
- Embed the role of mentor in the evaluation of senior faculty so that each individual will accept responsibility for overall success of the collective.

- Establish ongoing forums for new faculty to seek advice and discuss their needs.
- Create environments that honor collaboration rather than individualism.

Formal-Informal (isolated from, or interwoven with, the organization)

- To the greatest extent possible, clarify what is expected of individual faculty members and update it yearly.
- Conduct annual reviews with a candidate on the departmental level.
- Have the dean meet with each candidate every year to discuss problems and propose remedies.
- Provide arenas in which senior and junior colleagues can interact informally.
- Ensure that one individual is aware of the structure of faculty development for each tenure-track faculty member.

Random-Sequential (ambiguous or clearly ordered steps)

- Describe the kind of information needed for promotion and tenure files, and update it yearly.
- Develop a time frame for reviews and the format for its presentation.
- Develop a time frame for the specific steps of the promotion and tenure review.
- Discuss with candidates at their formal reviews what they will need for their files (e.g., outside letters of reference).
- State how and when a candidate will be told whether his or her candidacy is successful.

Fixed-Variable (specific or varying time frame)

- Ensure that when a candidate is initially employed by the organization he or she is informed in writing how many years, if any, have been granted toward tenure.
- Prior to the job offer and each yearly review, tell the candidate what he or she must do to be considered for "early tenure," "stopping the time clock," etc.
- Eliminate unnecessary evaluative steps (e.g., the department, college, and university ask for yearly lists of publications on three separate forms at three different times, when one form would suffice).
- Establish a clear process for how often and by what means a faculty member will have someone visit a class to observe his or her teaching.
- Recognize that because socialization is a variable process, different individuals will have special needs at different times.

Serial-Disjunctive (role models or no role models)

• Designate an individual to be in charge of mentoring.
• Create a plan for faculty development.
• Provide incentives for senior faculty to serve as mentors and consider how their performance in this capacity might be evaluated.
• Understand that individuals from underrepresented groups may be called on frequently to serve as role models, so take care not to overburden them with extraneous assignments.
• Make senior faculty aware that setting an example is an essential aspect of leadership.

Investiture-Divestiture (affirming or transforming individual characteristics)

• Develop seminars and workshops for senior faculty to help them understand how they might need to change their professional behavior as the composition of the faculty evolves.
• Establish an office on campus to orient faculty of color and facilitate their professional development. Such an office can also assist departments in creating strategies to recruit and retain faculty of color and to assess departmental climates for faculty of color periodically.
• Solicit feedback from tenure-track faculty about their needs and their opinion of faculty development.
• Involve junior faculty in decision making.
• Enable junior faculty to work as collaborators in research and teaching, rather than as neophytes.

Workload and Time

It is not uncommon for a newcomer to an organization to discover that there is "never enough time." The individual has usually moved to a new town, needs to orient his or her partner or family, must unpack books and files for the office, fill out a plethora of forms, and get on with the work for which he or she was hired. Consequently, young faculty who arrived on campus in August all too often find that they have no time to return to their research until summer vacation. However, when summer finally comes, they are exhausted emotionally and intellectually and find it difficult to pick up where they left off a year ago. Thus, another academic year begins with little progress having been made.

Furthermore, if new faculty have come to their positions directly from graduate school, they may initially think that faculty life will be like being a graduate student. All to soon, they discover that this is not the case. Graduate school is composed of hurdles: core requirements, candidacy examinations, qualifying examinations, and a dissertation. Although graduate study certainly presents its own set of dilemmas and problems, its structure is inherently different from a faculty situation in which a neophyte professor is told, "You have to publish, but I can't tell you how much. You have to teach, but I can't tell you what good teaching is, and you need to serve on committees, but not too many."

Probably for the first time in their lives, new faculty find themselves working in an atmosphere where no one will tell them what is expected. To be sure, the individual must teach his or her courses, but beyond that, what more is needed? Even if the organizational participants were to follow the steps outlined above, a high degree of ambiguity would still remain with regard to an individual's workload.

At the same time, individuals do have choices. They often have the option of accepting or declining a particular committee assignment. They usually have some leeway about how they structure their time on and off campus. They can stay up all night and do their research, or they can work through the weekends.

Our recommendation here is perhaps the most difficult to articulate, yet it is potentially the most important: New faculty should be made to understand that even though their work is inherently ambiguous, they are responsible for the structure of their professional lives. Because individuals want to succeed, we heard from faculty who felt they had no other choice than to work continuously. Our point is that if they want to do so, they may and they can; but they should realize that to take such a course of action is their decision. When a faculty member accepts the fact that he or she has control over time, there are two benefits. First, the individual will come to realize that he/she is in charge, not an abstract entity. Second, the individual may realize that options exist which do not entail spending sleepless nights for six years.

There are two principal ways that new faculty can learn how to structure their time. The department or division can provide all newly hired faculty with guides that explain how to navigate the waters of promotion and tenure. An alternative is to have a yearly workshop for senior faculty on their mentoring responsibilities and have them interpret those guides for their junior colleagues.

An example of the kind of guide to which we are referring is Robert Boice's *The New Faculty Member* (1992). Supported by years of longitudinal data, case histories, and interviews, Boice makes a compelling argument that structured faculty development programs can help new faculty be more productive in their writing and teaching. One example pertains to how faculty structure their day. It is not uncommon to hear an assistant professor say that he or she "devotes Thursdays" to writing. Presumably, the rest of the week is taken up with the myriad of other activities that constitute service and teaching: lesson plans, advisement, grading, committee work, and the like. But Boice contends persuasively that it is more productive for an individual to write every day, even if for only an hour. The individual may feel that no such "hours" exist, but in fact they do. If these hours are put to good use, the end result can be that a faculty member will complete an article or two a year more than a colleague who has not structured his or her time for such productivity. This is often precisely what one needs to achieve tenure or satisfaction with one's intellectual and professional progress.

Not only is information of this nature useful to tenure-track faculty members, it can also help mentors, departmental chairs, and deans to understand how to make faculty work less ambiguous. At a minimum, we recommend that all new faculty members should be provided with written materials on ways to improve faculty work. Senior colleagues should also be given these materials. Every year, a different facet of faculty work might be a subject for discussion by the full faculty. Virtually everyone in academe, for example, bemoans the snail's pace of decision-making by committees. The added problem for junior faculty is that time consumed by committee work is time away from activities that have greater relevance to their quest for tenure. Consequently, the structure of committee work is another topic for both junior and senior faculty to discuss.

The Promotion and Tenure Process

Although passing references to what should occur for promotion and tenure have appeared in other sections, we shall now discuss four critical points in the specific year of an individual's candidacy.

First, an individual should understand soon after joining the faculty what will be expected programmatically. Six years is a long time, and individuals often forget what committees they have served on, what papers they presented, or the comments they received from students or colleagues half a decade ago. Similarly, a list of potential outside reviewers is something that should be developed with care and consideration. As the interviews revealed, most individuals had not given much thought to this prior to the tenure year because they did not realize how important it was. The result was often a dossier that was not as strong as it might have been.

Second, candidates should not be betrayed by the system. If evaluations throughout the first five years have been positive, yet the candidate is denied tenure, then a mistake needs to be rectified. Formal evaluation can be helpful to an individual if it deals with areas for improvement as well as strengths. An organization that does not take evaluation seriously is apt to disable a candidate for tenure because he or she has never received adequate feedback. In effect, the greater blame goes to the organization, but the unsuccesful candidate must pay the penalty.

Third, we cannot emphasize enough that a unit must clarify what is expected of a candidate for tenure without bastardizing the process. That is, we do not believe that a candidate ought to be told exactly how many articles he or she needs for tenure, for this disregards the intellectual quality of the individual's work. By the same token, if an assistant professor is led to believe that a multi-authored article carries the same weight as a single-authored article, when in fact it does not, this is the result of a failure in communication. Consistent information widely shared is the best approach for avoiding such situations.

Fourth, a candidate should have a time frame for what is expected from him or her, and how decisions are reached. We heard from individuals who thought the dean made the final decision when that was not the case, and we heard from others who were told to rework their dossiers at the last minute. In large part, the individual quoted in chapter 3 who asked, "Why the mystery?" inspired this recommendation. It is to no one's advantage to have a process that is fraught with needless ambiguity. Individuals have the right to know about issues that affect their lives, and how and by whom decisions are made is essential information. Treating people with dignity requires that we ensure they understand the process; to do otherwise makes a mockery of an organization that presents itself as a community.

The Self-Reflective Organization

Building on the work of Adam Wildavsky (1972), Peter Ewell (1984) has called for participants in an organization to be "self-regarding." Ewell and Wildavsky contend that an effective and excellent institution is one in which individuals exhibit a concern for organizational processes and goals. We agree. All of the recommendations that we have made are not intended to serve as hard and fast rules to live by, but rather as strategies that may be of use to participants in an institution in their collective efforts to achieve excellence in academe. That notwithstanding, there are those who will have negative reactions to what we have reported and observed throughout this text: "It's naive to think a dean could spend his time talking with junior faculty," some will say. Others will add, "That scenario just doesn't fit my department." Still others will point out why our recommendations will have no effect: Faculty do not like to work collaboratively, senior colleagues do not have time to mentor others, and junior faculty do not know what they want, so helping them is virtually impossible. These are some actual comments we have heard.

We have sketched in this book problems that exist in a diverse array of colleges and universities. Faculty and administrators cannot wish these problems away and must face the fact that ignoring an issue does nothing to help resolve it. Indeed, at a time when academic institutions are beset with criticism about their nature and function, it is incumbent on all of us to be more self-reflective about the kind of institution we want to have. Is it acceptable for a new faculty member to be ignored because no one has given any thought to needs he or she may have? Is it convincing to claim that diversity is important if faculty of color can offer evidence that their work is undervalued or unappreciated? Do we have the right to call ourselves a community when any sense of social obligation to one another is absent? Obviously not.

Optimistically, we have offered strategies for changing the world as we know it. Our recommendations have a dual purpose. Our intent in this section has been to fulfill the first objective: to improve the world as we know it. But as we enter into discussions that compel us to be self-reflective, a second objective begins to materialize: to envision what we might yet construct. What "new lands" might we discover if we "launch out on to unknown seas"?

The Academic World as It Might Be

Reviewing the Data

In none of the interviews did individuals mention academic freedom as a right they felt they enjoyed. Their silence on the subject is understandable because they did not have tenure. In essence, if tenure protects academic freedom, then those who do not have it are not protected. Thus, to call for dramatic changes in the tenure system on the basis of interviews with the untenured may be misguided.

The AAUP, which is the leading advocate for tenure, has steadfastly maintained that tenure and academic freedom go hand in hand; to change tenure would threaten academic freedom. In an article recently republished, for example, Van Waes alluded to a commission of twenty years ago that underscored

the vital relationship of tenure to the freedom of the academy, emphasized that no proposed substitute for tenure offered equivalent guarantees of that freedom, and ringingly reaffirmed the necessity of retaining the present system. (1994, p 86)

Such "ringing reaffirmation" is as disheartening to us as the scorched-earth rhetoric of the conservatives. The conservatives long to return to a golden age of academe that never really existed. Proponents of tenure demand that the status quo be maintained. Neither approach is adequate to meet the challenges that colleges and universities will face in the twenty-first century. Critical postmodernism teaches us that contexts do change, that individual and group identities do matter. To assume that one structure is acceptable regardless of time, culture, place, or identity is a mistake. The chair of a university department expressed the need for change as follows:

> A number of us are grumbling and saying we have to do better. We take talented people, and they have all these pressures that we put on them. One of the things we have been talking about is to do away with the seven-year system. But it would put us in variance with other schools, and since tenure is sort of a competitive kind of thing, nobody wants to be the first to change it in any way. Some of us are saying, "Look, people get sick, people have children, people's parents get sick, and they have to take time out" . . . all kinds of personal things affect faculty lives. We could say, "We will give you ten years, or you can come up whenever you want to, whenever you feel you are ready."

Our concern remains with the focus of this book: socialization and community in academe. The data show that typical junior faculty are socialized not to take intellectual risks and not to question assumptions, because doing this might impede their efforts to have their work published. Faculty members admitted they were socialized to meet norms that had little, if anything, to do with the protection or advancement of academic freedom. In the implicit definition of community, competition rather than cooperation is emphasized. Recall, for example, the individual with a number of multi-authored articles to his credit who learned belatedly that collaboration was not regarded as a sufficient indicator of scholarship. He was then obliged to concentrate on individual work to justify tenure. Remember the faculty member who said he never felt good about having an article published because the comment was always, "And now what?" And the individual who received a sizable five-year grant but had never been congratulated by her colleagues for this accomplishment.

We are also uncomfortable with the criteria that have developed with regard to tenure. If tenure protects academic freedom, then what, if anything, does the quality of one's service have to do with its attainment? Colleges and universities have developed a system in which faculty members are judged on the basis of abstract topics. If the community of elders decide that the initiates are competent in these topics, they are granted tenure. And yet, considering how well someone serves on committees in order to determine if he or she deserves the protection of academic freedom seems as illogical as deciding that someone is a good baseball player and therefore he or she should become governor of the state.

Similarly, the defense of tenure as a protection of academic freedom is often decontextualized and ahistorical. Tenure originated in this century. To assume that this system must be perpetuated out of respect for tradition is unreasonable when academe is entering a period that demands great change. Tenure is a structure or system, as are departments, academic units, and administrative bodies. All of these entities are dynamic, fluid, and capable of change; the reification of such structures obscures and denigrates the actual ideas that they have been created to serve.

That is, academic freedom is a concept that was the hallmark of superior academic institutions long before tenure came into existence. As O'Toole has noted, "Academic freedom is guaranteed not by the tenure system but by a thousand years of Anglo-American tradition. . . . The true source of academic freedom from Socrates to Scopes has been the courage of individual scholars." (1994, 85) In this light, academic freedom in academe, like free speech in society, is protected not by a bureaucratic system, but by the community. As we noted in chapter 1, from the intellectual perspective of critical postmodernism, how the academy thinks about representational practices such as academic freedom should be reconsidered. How is it protected today, and how is this different from the way things were fifty years ago? In the position advocated here, the community is genuinely committed to the idea of democracy and devoted to its protection, not the structure on which it is built. Different social and historical contexts may indicate structural changes are needed, and we contend that facile support for the status quo is stagnation at best and regression at worst. It is irrational because structures inevitably change, and it is detrimental because such entrenched closed-mindedness has eroded public confidence in the academy. Because of this, conservative critics have directed their broadsides at individuals rather than at a structure in need of renovation, and members of the academy have avoided honest dialogues about the direction their communities should take in the twenty-first century.

The advancement of knowledge or the relationship of higher learning to society are ideas that were supported in academe in the past. Prior to the twentieth century, academic departments such as we know them did not exist. Postsecondary institutions have vacillated about engagement with or distance from society. College and university participants are currently revising their definitions of knowledge in ways that will undoubtedly transform departmental and college-wide structures. Postsecondary institutions also appear to be moving toward greater engagement with society.

Our point is that we must not confuse an idea with a structure; tenure is not academic freedom. At the same time, we ought not to recommend doing away with tenure if we have not thought out what structure or system will replace it to protect the ideal of the community—academic freedom.

Our concern about tenure is derived from the data. We have heard from individuals who used as a goal not so much to "advance knowledge," but to "obtain tenure." This is understandable because individuals are socialized into a system that, despite all rhetoric glorifying the former, attaches more importance to the latter. We are suggesting that the tenure process should inspire thoughtful dialogue about institutional and individual protections of academic freedom, but it does not. Instead, it is a six-year-long rite of passage intended to socialize neophytes in how to behave as members of the academic tribe.

The consequences of the tenure system are that junior and senior faculty members alike become mired in a bureaucracy that confounds dialogues of respect about individual or group difference, and sidesteps honest consideration of what constitutes the academic community. Individuals work to achieve high marks on student evaluations, or to have an article published in an "A" journal. In effect, the professorate has bought into credentialism even though the relationship between tenure and the protection of academic freedom has become increasingly obscure. The interviews also offer insight into a cronyism that prevents individuals from debating ideas; instead, junior faculty are likely to feel that, like good children, they "should be seen and not heard." They may attempt to curry favor with senior colleagues in order to garner external or internal support for their candidacy, and they are almost inevitably placed in competition with one another. Regrettably, the "marketplace of ideas" has taken on a particularly pernicious interpretation that accentuates hyper-individualism rather than collective dialogue and debate.

In an ironic twist, supporters of academic freedom have argued that the collegiality of academe would be lost without tenure. One wonders if these proponents have spoken with junior faculty about collegiality, or if they have heard how it is perceived by women or faculty of color. This is not to suggest that tenure is the source of all academic ills; but most assuredly it is not the remedy, either.

Further, some form of evaluation should exist, regardless of whether it has anything to do with academic freedom. That is, even if an institution protects a faculty member's academic freedom, this does not indicate that the individual is a good teacher, researcher, or committee member. However, as the interviews indicated, involvement in the tenure process paradoxically left one little time for professional development. We heard from individuals who knew what their shortcomings were, but felt they did not need to nor have to change in order to attain promotion and tenure. The majority of the interviewees felt that service was irrelevant to tenure as long as one maintained token involvement. Research in the sciences and professions often depended not so much on the superior intellect of an individual, but on his or her ability to obtain outside funding. Research in general had at least as much to do with the production of publishable material as with the quality of one's ideas.

In essence, the system as it is now configured seems doubly flawed. On one hand, tenure neither protects nor advances the concept for which it was intended—academic freedom. Tenure and academic freedom are not mutually supportive, but only tangentially related. On the other hand, tenure often constitutes an insurmountable obstacle to initiatives for the improvement of teaching, research, and service.

To be sure, violations of academic freedom still occur. Some individuals have enjoyed the support of tenure as they advance toward the frontiers of knowledge. Without a structure, some of them would undoubtedly have been dismissed or marginalized in their institution. But is tenure the only system that can protect members of the academic community?

An Organizational Framework for Excellence

If we were to assume for the moment that tenure did not exist in its present form, one would be hard pressed to believe we would invent the same system. Yesterday's solutions are not adequate to meet today's challenges. However, we do not intend to enter into a discussion about changing the tenure system *tabula rasa*; whatever we might propose would either seem utopian and farfetched, or such a massive undertaking that few individuals will consider the goal achievable or the effort worthwhile.

However, organizational alternatives that protect academic freedom without tenure do exist. For example, Hampshire College and Evergreen State College, a private and a public institution respectively, have long-term contracts that the faculty believe maintain academic freedom and intellectual independence. We mention these two institutions because even though they are relatively new they have earned reputations for their faculties' creative and independent thought. If faculty who regularly question norms can survive and prosper without tenure, then such systems at least deserve investigation.

Similarly, others have suggested that if the tenure system were abolished then faculties would turn en masse to unionization (O'Toole 1994). The point is entirely empirical, of course, but it is unreasonable to refuse to consider a change—overhauling tenure—merely because another change—unionization—might occur. There are positive and negative examples of unions, and to assume that unionization is an absolute good or evil is unreasonable. Rather, there should first be a discussion about changes that might streamline tenure, and what kind of system might be considered to replace it.

In the United States, we are obsesssed with evaluation. We eschew explicit discussions of educational philosophy, opting instead for a system for the evaluation of the academic community. Often there is a good reason for evaluation. Institutions should have goals relevant to what their students are supposed to learn, and the goals should be articulated so clearly that everyone understands them. Similarly, faculties should undergo some form of evaluation periodically so that they can say with confidence that they are effective teachers and researchers.

Yet what has occurred is that evaluation has usurped the position of the institutional philosophy. Evaluation is now regarded an end rather than a means. What we are suggesting is that the administration and faculty need to concentrate more fully on procedural issues. Merely to sit in the back of a room and write a report on someone's teaching that goes into a tenure file does little, if anything, to improve an individual's teaching. It does, however, fulfill an evaluative requirement. To deny tenure because an individual does not have the requisite number of publications involves no consideration of the intellectual merit of his or her publications. Furthermore, to insist that an individual serve on committees in order to demonstrate good citizenship equates faculty meetings with democracy. Community participation involves more than sitting in a room so that one's attendance can be duly noted.

If we were to concentrate on process, we would find ourselves considering issues such as how every member of the teaching staff might improve his or her teaching. We would welcome every opportunity to discuss our scholarly activities and advice, support and criticism from our colleagues. Moreover, service would become a central aspect of how we relate to one another. Service in a democracy is what makes governance possible; it is not the bloated bureaucratic nightmare that consumes an individual's time and stands in the way of the creation of communities of difference.

The majority will maintain that faculty still need to be evaluated. While we agree with this essentially, we also contend that the American obsession with evaluation prevents meaningful discussions about what individuals believe, and how they will decide what is important. Discussions about evaluation all too often serve to sort, filter and dismiss individuals; the tenure decision is the prime example of this.

Other possibilities exist, but to consider them we must reframe the discussion away from evaluation and toward process. It is common knowledge that for decades, many large Japanese companies employed individuals who work for the same company throughout their entire career. The Japanese system is not one in which an employee is required either to move up or to move on to another organization, yet few would argue that it does not reward excellence and effectiveness. For the common good, the Japanese often work with their less competent colleagues to help them improve their performance rather than grading or dismissing them.

Let us be clear about the following. We are not recommending that all institutions abolish tenure and replace it with a system akin to that of Hampshire or Evergreen State. Nor are we saying that all faculties should unionize. Furthermore, we are not arguing that personnel should be hired with tenure for life, as is the policy in many Japanese companies. What we are suggesting is that alternatives do exist, and members of a community need to consider them.

Thus, in order to reconceptualize higher education, community must move away from positions that perpetuate the status quo or purposeless evaluation, and engage in critical discussions of institutional values and philosophy. Academics also need to consider what kind of work individuals should do. To assist faculty members in their rethinking of faculty work, faculty rewards, and faculty interaction, we offer three overarching strategies.

Develop a Comparative and Historical Awareness

To assume that tenure is an absolute that protects academic freedom is mistaken from a historical perspective, as well as a comparative one. Tenure is a twentieth-century invention. Institutions currently exist without tenure, yet their faculty are allowed to engage in productive and provocative dialogues.

Far too often the powers that be in academe behave as if there were only one solution, when actually there are many. The ability to understand academic work from a contemporary and sociocultural perspective enables decision makers to give serious consideration to alternatives that might otherwise have been discarded.

Articulate the Mission of the Institution

Defining institutional purpose is a very risky undertaking. Common wisdom would have it that lofty vision statements are too easy and too time-consuming, and we agree. Presidential pronouncements about the purpose of the institution often inspire derisive comments; a year-long committee formed to define the future of the institution often produces a bland document that goes unchallenged and is placed on the shelf to gather dust as soon as the committee is disbanded.

We are not speaking, however, of a symbolic gesture that has only a vague connection to the basic workings of the institution. Indeed, one major problem with the tenure system and socialization process is that the community is unsure of how individuals should spend their time. Should faculty "waste" time on committee work? If an engineer is unsuccessful in her efforts to obtain a grant, should this mean that she will not be granted tenure? If teaching is important, then how much should one person do, and how will it be evaluated?

We contend that all of these questions are philosophical in nature. As José Ortega y Gasset has written, "The root of university reform is a complete formulation of its purpose. Any alteration or adjustment of this house of ours unless it starts by reviewing the problem of its mission—clearly, decisively, truthfully—will be love's labors lost." (1944, p 28) From this perspective, the mission of an organization amounts to more than a presidential pronouncement on Faculty Day. Furthermore, organizational change cannot be achieved by tinkering with the fringe elements of the system.

To question the mission of an institution, decision makers must become involved not simply in internal discussions about where the institution should go; they must also look to the external environment for indications of what society has to offer and what society expects. When we look to the environment, for example, we find that it is unreasonable to expect that junior faculty in all but the most prestigious institutions will be able to obtain as much outside funding as their predecessors. There is every indication that federal funding of research will decrease, and if this is so, administrators and senior faculty need to reconsider what they may reasonably expect from their junior colleagues.

Similarly, postsecondary educational institutions also have a symbiotic relationship with society. During some eras, colleges and universities maintained a distance from local and national contexts, and at other times they have been much closer. At present, not only are state legislatures and national commissions asking for closer relationships; parents and students are also demanding it. If teaching is to be accorded greater value, then faculty members who spend the greater part of their time conducting research need to reconsider their priorities. Moreover, if change is to be lasting, then it must be reinforced through the reward system. But first, the institution's participants must reach an agreement about their mission. To contend that the institution values teaching, for example, yet rewards someone who conducts research at the expense of teaching, is illogical. To reform a tenure system so that individuals concentrate on continuous improvement of their teaching and scholarship is in keeping with what we are suggesting.

Foment Critical Dialogue

We have argued that while tenure came into being to protect academic freedom, in the late twentieth century faculty members are now socialized to a community that accords privileges to some and silences others. The consensual model of the academic community enforces symbolic codes that do not encourage individuals to take intellectual risks, to disagree with one another, or to challenge accepted notions or ideas. Systems and structures are populated, supported, and enforced by individuals. If leadership is to some extent achieved by example, then those in positions of power need to create arenas in which public disagreement can occur in a provocative and positive manner. Only this can protect individuals who have the desire and will to challenge commonly accepted norms in public.

Our point here is that when administrators and faculty members begin to consider changing a tenure system, the protection of academic freedom will rightfully be an immediate concern. In an intellectual community such discussions should occur on two levels. First, one should seriously question whether academic freedom actually exists at the institution to the extent that individuals assume it does (Tierney 1993b). Academic freedom should be central to any institutional discussion of proposed change, insofar as free speech is a respected precept within. However, individuals and groups should not simply talk about academic freedom as an abstract concept; they should be encouraged to experiment, to think creatively, and to seek to break scientific norms.

An organization that rewards change is different from one that sanctions violations of norms. To perpetuate norms demands one kind of institutional climate, and to encourage innovation requires another. As the twenty-first century approaches, we have ventured to suggest that a structure that helped create first-rate institutions is now in need of change. What was once innovative—the creation of a promotion and tenure system—has become rigid and inflexible and does not meet the needs and requirements of a socially responsible institution of the future.

No maps chart the territory we are to encounter in the next century. What we discover is unlikely to be a Garden of Eden. Our thesis throughout this book has been that those of us in postsecondary institutions need to develop greater self-referentiality as we begin to create communities of difference that will be populated by individuals and groups quite different from those of the past. Academic structures will be different as well. What academic communities will look like in fifty years, and what norms individuals will be socialized to, are open questions. The intent of this book has been to create awareness that the answers to such questions will be found in the hearts and minds of progressive members of the academic community who are ready, willing, and able to accept the challenges of the future.

Appendix A

This study was carried out in twelve colleges and universities throughout the United States. The profile of participating institutions is as follows: Carnegie classification

Carnegie classification
Research I	3
Doctoral II	1
Masters I	3
Baccalaureate I	4
Baccalaureate II	1

Control
Public	4
Private	8

Size
10,000 and higher	4
5,001–9,999	2
5,000 and under	6

Six institutions were visited twice in 1992–93 and a second time in 1993–94, the remaining six institutions were visited just once. At each institution we interviewed assistant professors who were in various stages of progress in the tenure track. We also interviewed the chairs of their departments, members of promotion and tenure committees, as well as academic deans, provosts and members of their staff. The semi-structured interview protocol is shown in Appendix B. The majority of the interviews were audio-taped and transcribed.

Overall, we interviewed 202 assistant professors, 54 department chairs and deans, and 14 provosts or their associates.

The characteristics of the assistant professors were as follows:

Sex
Women	99
Men	103
TOTAL	202

149

Race/Ethnicity

African American	22
Latino/Latina	15
Asian American	6
American Indian	2
Foreign	15
White	142
TOTAL	202

Discipline Areas

Liberal Arts and Sciences	122
Business	38
Education	12
Engineering	22
Communication	8
TOTAL	202

Appendix B

Institutional Socialization and Faculty Peer Review

Protocol

I am engaged in a study that is trying to understand how new faculty are socialized in their university, college and department. In particular, I am trying to understand what institutions can do to improve the climate for pretenure faculty. Let me begin with some broad questions.

 I. History
1. How long have you been here?
2. Why did you choose to come here?
3. What were some alternatives?
4. Demographic Data:
 II. Being interviewed and prior to coming here
1. What was the interview like for your position?
2. What were your initial impressions about the institution prior to coming here?
3. What did you think was expected of you?
4. Who communicated with you prior to coming here?
III. Present
1. How would you describe the institution's mission?
2. Tell me about when you first arrived? (What was it like)
3. Was (and is) there any type of (on-going) orientation?
4. What's the climate like? (institution, college, department)
5. What activities make the greatest demand on you?
6. What do you enjoy most (least) about your job?
7. Talk about your colleagues.
8. Tell me who is a productive colleague (and why).
9. How has your perception changed about this place and what's expected of you?
10. How did you learn to do your job?

151

11. Is there anything you would like to spend greater time on?
12. How do you know if you're doing a good job?
13. What advice would you give to a new faculty member coming here?

IV. Story-telling
    1. Tell me a story about your arrival here.
    2. Tell me a story about conflict you experience(d.)
    3. Tell me a story about your department.
    4. Tell me a story about what's it like to be a (woman, minority).
    5. Tell me a story about how people interact here.

Bibliography

Aiken, S.H., Anderson, K., Dinnerstein, M., Lensink, J., & MacCorquodale, P. (1987). Trying transformations: Curriculum integration and the problem of resistance. *Signs*, *12*(2), 255–275.

Aisenberg, N., & Harrington, M. (1988). *Women of academe: Outsiders in the sacred grove.* Amherst, MA: The University of Massachusetts Press.

American Association of University Professors (1985). Academic freedom and tenure: Statement of principles, 1940. In Finkelstein, M.J. (Ed.), *ASHE Reader on faculty and faculty issues in colleges and universities*, 143–145. Lexington, MA: Ginn Press.

Astin, H.S., & Davis, D.E. (1985). Research productivity across the life and career cycles: Facilitators and barriers for women. In Fox, M.F. (Ed.), *Scholarly writing and publishing: Issues, problems and solutions.* Boulder: Westview Press.

Austin, A.E. (1990). Faculty cultures, faculty values. In Tierney, W.G. (Ed.), *New Directions for Institutional Research: No. 68. Assessing Academic Climates and Cultures.* San Francisco: Jossey-Bass.

Becher, T. (1987). The disciplinary shaping of the profession. In Clark, B.R. (Ed.), *The academic profession: National, disciplinary, and institutional settings.* Berkeley and Los Angeles: University of California Press.

Bennett, W.J. (1984). *To reclaim a legacy: A report on the humanities in higher education.* Washington, D.C.: National Endowment for the Humanities.

Bensimon, E.M. (1992). Lesbian existence and the challenge to normative constructions of the academy. *Journal of Education*, *174*(3), 98–113.

Bentley, R.J., & Blackburn, R.T. (1992). Two decades of gains for female faculty? *Teachers College Record*, *93*(4), 697–709.

Bloom, A. (1987). *The closing of the American mind: How higher education has failed democracy and impoverished the souls of today's students.* New York: Simon & Schuster.

Boice, R. (1992). *The new faculty member: Supporting and fostering professional development.* San Francisco: Jossey-Bass.

Bourdieu, P. (1977). *Outline of a theory of practice* (R. Nice, Trans.) Cambridge, MA: Cambridge University Press.

Bowen, H.R., & Schuster, J.H. (1986). *American professors: A national resource imperiled.* New York: Oxford University Press.

Boyer, E.L. (1990). *Scholarship reconsidered: Priorities of the professoriate.* Princeton, NJ: The Carnegie Foundation for the Advancement of Teaching.

Bronstein, P., Rothblum, E., & Solomon, S. (1993). Ivy halls and glass walls: Barriers to academic careers for women and ethnic minorities. In Gainen, J., & Boice, R. (Eds.), *New Directions for Teaching and Research: Vol. 53. Building a diverse faculty.* San Francisco: Jossey-Bass.

Clark, B.R. (1983). *The higher education system: Academic organization in cross-national perspective.* Berkeley: University of California Press.

———. (1987). *The academic life.* Princeton, NJ: Carnegie Foundation for the Advancement of Teaching.

Clark, S.M., & Corcoran, M. (1986). Perspectives on the professional socialization of women faculty: A case of accumulative disadvantage? *Journal of Higher Education, 57*(1), 20–43.

D'Souza, D. (1991). *Illiberal education: The politics of race and sex on campus.* New York: The Free Press.

Dwyer, M.M., Flynn, A.A., & Inman, P.S. (1991). Differential progress of women faculty: Status 1980–1990. In Smart, J. (Ed.), *Handbook of Theory and Research, 7,* 173–222.

Elliot, O. (1937). *Stanford University: The first twenty-five years.* Stanford, CA: Stanford University Press.

Ewell, P. (1984). *The self-regarding institution: Information for excellence.* Boulder, CO: National Center for Higher Education Management Systems.

Fairweather, J.S. (1993). Academic values and faculty rewards. *The Review of Higher Education, 17*(1), 43–68.

Fox, M.F. (1985). *Scholarly writing and publishing: Issues, problems, and solutions.* Boulder & London: Westview Press.

Geiger, R.L. (1993). *Research and relevant knowledge: American research universities since World War II.* New York: Oxford University Press.

Giroux, H.A. (1988). Border pedagogy in the age of postmodernism. *Journal of Education, 170*(3), 162–181.

Gumport, P.J. (1990). Feminist scholarship as a vocation. *Higher Education, 20*(3), 231–243.

Hofstadter, R., & Metzger, W.P. (1955). *The development of academic freedom in the United States.* New York: Columbia University Press.

hooks, b. (1989). *Talking back: Thinking feminist, thinking black.* Boston: South End Press.

Jacoby, R. (1987). *The last intellectuals: American culture in the age of academe.* New York: Basic Books.

Kimball, R. (1990). *Tenured radicals: How politics has corrupted our higher education.* New York: Harper & Row

Luke, C., & Gore, J. (Eds.), (1990). *Feminisms and critical pedagogy.* New York: Routledge.

McCart, C.L. (1991). *Using a cultural lens to explore faculty perceptions of academic freedom.* Unpublished doctoral dissertation, Pennsylvania State University, University Park.

Merton, R.K. (1957). *Social theory and social structure.* Glencoe, IL: The Free Press.

Metzger, W. (1955). *Academic freedom in the age of the university.* New York: Columbia University Press.

Moses, Y.T. (1989). *Black women in academe: Issues and strategies.* Washington, D.C.: Association of American Colleges, Project on the Status and Education of Women.

National Research Council (1993). *U.S. doctorate survey.* Washington, D.C.

Nieves-Squires, S. (1991). *Hispanic women: Making their presence on campus less tenuous.* Washington: Association of American Colleges, Project on the Status and Education of Women.

Ollman, B. (1983). Academic freedom in America today: A Marxist view. In C. Kaplan & E. Schrecker (Eds.), *Regulating the intellectuals,* 45–59. New York: Praeger.

Ortega y Gassett, J. (1944). *Mission of the university.* New York: Norton.

O'Toole, J. (1994). Tenure: A conscientious objection. *Change, 26*(3), 78–89.

Padilla, A.M. (1994). Ethnic minority scholars, research, and mentoring: Current and future issues. *Educational Researcher, 23*(4), 24–27.

Ravitch, D. (1990). Multiculturalism. *The American Scholar, 59*(3), 337–354.

Rochlin, M. (1993, May). The mathematics of discrimination. *Los Angeles Times Magazine,* May 2.

Ross, E. (1936). *Seventy years of it.* New York: Appleton-Century Co.

Rudolph, F. (1962). *The American college and university: A history.* New York: Vintage Books

Sandler, B.R. (1986). *The campus climate revisited: A chilly one for women faculty, administrators, and graduate students.* Washington, D.C.: Association of American Colleges.

Schrecker, E. (1983). Academic freedom: The historical view. In Kaplan, C. & Schrecker, E. (Eds.), *Regulating the intellectuals,* 25–43. New York: Praeger.

Schuster, M., & Van Dyne, S. (1984). Placing women in the liberal arts: Stages of curriculum transformation. *Harvard Educational Review, 54*(4), 413–428.

Slaughter, S. (1980). The danger zone: Academic freedom and civil liberties. *The ANNALS of the American academy of political and social science, 448,* 4661.

Sowell, T. (1992). The scandal of college tuition. *Commentary, 95,* 23–26.

———. (1993). *Inside American education: The decline, the deception, the dogmas.* New York: The Free Press.

Sykes, C.J. (1988). *ProfScam: Professors and the demise of higher education.* New York: St. Martin's Press.

Tierney, W.G. (1993a). *Building communities of difference: Higher education in the twenty-first century.* Westport, CT: Bergin & Garvey.

———. (1993b). Academic freedom and the parameters of knowledge. *Harvard Educational Review, 63*(2), 143–160.

Tierney, W.G., & Rhoads, R.A. (1993). *Enhancing promotion, tenure and beyond: Faculty socialization as a cultural process.* ASHE-ERIC Higher Education Report No. 93-6. Washington, D.C.: The George Washington University.

Turner, C.S, & Thompson, J.R. (1993). Socializing women doctoral students: Minority and majority experiences. *The Review of Higher Education, 16*(3), 355–370.

Van Alstyne, W. (1985). Tenure: A summary, explanation, and "defense". In Finkelstein, M.J. (Ed.), *ASHE Reader on faculty and faculty issues in colleges and universities.* (pp. 146–154). Lexington, MA: Ginn Press.

Van Maanen, J., & Schein, E.H. (1979). Toward a theory of organizational socialization. In B.M. Staw (Ed.), *Research in Organizational Behavior (Vol. 1)*, 209–264. Greenwich, CT: JAI Press.

Van Waes, R. (1994). The debate on tenure. *Change, 26*(3), 86.

Veysey, L.R. (1965). *The emergence of the American university.* Chicago: The University of Chicago Press.

West, C. (1990). The new cultural politics of difference. *October, 53,* 93–109.

Wildavsky, A. (1972). The self-evaluating organization. *Public Administration Review, 32,* 509–520.

Index

A

Academe
  community and, 1–20, 140
  culture and, 1–20
  perspectives of, 1–20
  socialization and, 140
  women faculty and, 87
Academic bricoleurs, 19
Academic community
  academic structures and, 148
  difference and, 16, 37, 129, 144, 147
  evaluation of, 142–144
  interpretation of, 14
  socialization and, 21–42
  tenure and, 21–42
Academic freedom
  faculty perceptions of, 26
  function of, 25
  limits of, 25
  socialization and, 140
  tenure and, 6–10, 22–24, 27, 35, 139, 143, 147
Academic structures
  academic communities and, 148
  comparison of, 34
  ideology, 13
  organization of, 15
  postmodern interpretations, 13
  sexism and, 97
  symbols and, 13
  women-centered, 95–102
Academy
  conservatism and, 6–9
  critical postmodernism and, 12–17
  cultural taxation and, 103–124
  culture and, 120
  ethnicity and, 103–124
  liberal humanism and, 9
  minority faculty and, 120
  postmodernism and, 141
  present state of, 5
  race and, 103–124
  socialization and, 103–124
  structures of, 140
  triple functions of, 10
Accommodation
  "mom" work and, 85–89, 101
  "smile" work and, 83–85, 101
Acculturation, 18
Affirmative action, 78, 96–97, 103–104, 118
American Association of University Professors, 25
American Economics Association, 24
American Political Science Association, 24
American Sociological Society, 24
Anticipatory socialization, 37, 44, 48, 79, 125–126, 129–131. *See also* Socialization
Association of American Colleges, 25

B

Board of Trustees, 32–34
Bricoleur, 19

C

Career Development Plan, 29
Collective socialization, 38, 58, 133–134. *See also* Socialization
College financing, 5. *See also* financial issues
Collegiality, 89–90
Committees, 2–3, 27, 31, 33, 75, 98, 129
Commodification, 117
Communities of difference, 16, 129, 144, 147
  socialization and, 37

SUNY SERIES
FRONTIERS IN EDUCATION
List of Titles